Recent Research in Psychology
Applied Behavioral Science

Marta L. Axelson   David Brinberg

A Social-Psychological Perspective on Food-Related Behavior

Springer-Verlag
New York Berlin Heidelberg
London Paris Tokyo Hong Kong

𝒫

Marta L. Axelson
East Schodak, NY 12603, USA

David Brinberg
State University of New York
Marketing Department/School of Business
Albany, NY 12222, USA

Library of Congress Catologing-in-Publication Data

Axelson, Marta L.
          A social-psychological perspective on food-related behavior / by Marta L.
Axelson & David Brinberg.
                    p. cm.--(Recent research in psychology. Applied behavioral science)
          Includes bibliographical references.
          ISBN 0-387-97095-9
          1. Food--Psychological aspects. I. Brinberg, David. II. Title. III. Series.
          [DNLM: 1. Feeding Behavior. 2. Social Behavior. 3. Socioeconomic Factors.
GT 2850 A969s]
          TX357.A94 1989
          152.5--dc20
          DNLM/DLC   89-21617
          for Library of Congress

Printed on acid-free paper.

Camera-ready copy prepared by the authors.
Printed and bound by Edwards Bros., Inc., Ann Arbor, Michigan.
Printed in the United States of America.

9 8 7 6 5 4 3 2 1

ISBN 0-387-97095-9 Springer-Verlag New York Berlin Heidelberg
ISBN 3-540-97095-9 Springer-Verlag Berlin Heidelberg New York

7/16/90

Authors' Note

The information in this monograph is intended for two general professional groups who are interested in food-related behavior. The first group includes professionals like those in the fields of food and nutrition. These professionals emerge from their training conversant in concepts and methods commonly used in the natural sciences, but often have limited experience with the concepts and methods used in the social sciences. The second group includes professionals like those in psychology, consumer behavior, and health education. These professionals are conversant in the concepts and methods commonly used in the social sciences, but often have limited experience in the application of these concepts and methods to food-related behavior. The major aim of this monograph is to discuss issues surrounding the definitions and measurements of food-related behavior and its determinants.

We would like to thank Joanne Guthrie for reading parts of this monograph and Julein Axelson for reading the entire manuscript. Both provided useful comments. Rudi Pritzl deserves a special thanks for producing the final copy of the monograph.

M.L.A.
D.B.

East Schodack, NY
The University at Albany - SUNY
March 1989

Contents

1

Everyone seems to be an expert--at least when it comes to eating. People can tell you, without much hesitation, about what foods they eat, why they eat certain foods and avoid others, when they eat, and with whom they eat. In general, they can provide you with a lot of information about their eating patterns. In fact, they can be rather emphatic about the entire subject. As the evidence accumulates for the relationship between the occurrence of many diseases (e.g., adult-onset diabetes mellitus, hyperlipidemia, and colon cancer) and many food consumption patterns, health professionals are beginning to realize that health promotion is as important as the time-honored goal of disease treatment. The emphasis on health promotion has induced professionals in fields outside traditional medicine to focus research and education efforts on food-related behavior. Professionals in food and nutrition, health education, social marketing, and psychology as well as others have intensified their efforts to find ways to promote beneficial eating patterns in the general population. Modifying people's food-related behaviors, however, requires an understanding of why people eat what they eat. The good news for health professionals is that people are interested in food and nutrition, and they can tell us a lot about how they think, feel, and act in relation to food. The bad news, however, is that when people perceive themselves as knowledgeable about a topic, they are less receptive to new information and less likely to modify their behaviors.

To study a person's food-related behavior is to study the interaction of a person's social, psychological, and biological needs. Not surprising, then, is to find scientists in the social, psychological, and biological sciences examining the determinants of food-related behavior, and to find their work scattered across many journals. Although both social and biological factors influence people's food-related behavior, the focus of this monograph is on social-psychological determinants of behavior. The point-of-view used in this monograph can be characterized as social psychological in that concepts are presented from the perspective of their effect on the food-related behaviors of the individual. For example, a social psychologist views the effect of culture on behavior as mediated through its effect on the beliefs, preferences, and attitudes of the individual, whereas an anthropologist views culture as a direct determinant (explanation) of an individual's behavior. Psychosocial variables are thought to reflect the individual's internal state, and commonly examined variables include knowledge, beliefs, and attitudes. Sociodemographic variables are thought to reflect an individual's access to socially-mediated activities: these variable often are called external variables and include income, ethnicity, age, and the like.

The prominent social concepts and methods used to study people's food-related behavior and its determinants are examined in this monograph. The discussion begins in Chapter 2 with an examination of the variety of measures used to study behavior. Food-related behavior has been conceptualized in two general ways: as a behavior and as an outcome of behavior. Behavioral measurements include food choices, food purchases, and types and amounts of food consumed. A commonly measured outcome of behavior is nutrient intake.

The concepts of attitudes, beliefs, and knowledge and the issues related to their measurement are examined in Chapter 3. In Chapter 4, food preferences are discussed and compared to the concept of attitudes. Interest in these psychosocial determinants of food-related behavior has grown out of the realization that the sociodemographic determinants (Chapter 5) accounted for a fairly low proportion of the variance observed in individuals' food consumption patterns. That is, even though individuals had the resources with which to obtain a good diet, they displayed food consumption patterns that, from the nutritionists' point of view, needed improving. Nutrition and health educators hypothesized that if individuals increased their knowledge of nutrition and modified their beliefs and attitudes, then desirable changes in their food-related behaviors would result. Thus, information was required about the determinants of an individuals' eating patterns (how they behave), their knowledge (what they think) and their attitudes (what they feel).

Some decision-making models that attempt to specify the relationships among beliefs, attitudes, and behavior are reviewed and contrasted in Chapter 6. A description of how these models have been applied or could be applied to the analysis of food-related behavior is provided. The final chapter is about professionals and consumers' food classification systems. Two aspects of professionals' food classification systems are examined--the cognitive component and the guidance (or behavioral) component. The role of these components in the development and use of food guides is discussed, followed by an examination of the concepts and methods used to study consumers' classification systems.

We know that what we eat affects our health. Thus, we need to understand why we eat the foods that we do to better understand how we can develop and maintain dietary practices conducive to good health. The remainder of this monograph examines some of those factors that affect what we eat.

2

The foundation for understanding food-related behavior and its determinants rests on the definition and measurement of behavior. Food-related behavior has been defined and measured in a variety of ways. Each definition and its concomitant measurement possesses different assumptions, potential strengths, and inherent weaknesses. In the following sections, various approaches for defining and measuring food-related behavior are discussed. We will present a framework for organizing and comparing these approaches and will examine various criteria for evaluating the quality of the measurements of food-related behavior.

Defining Food-Related Behavior

One simple approach is to define food-related behavior as what people do; that is, people's actions toward food. This simple definition, however, aggregates (and treats as the same) a wide variety of actions toward food. People can consume food, sell food, buy food, throw food, use food as a weapon (as in poison food), and perform a host of other actions toward foods. Four behaviors--choice, purchase, consumption, and nutrient intake--will be examined here because each has been used as the criterion variable by researchers studying food-related behavior.

These four behaviors may be viewed as a set of sequential steps that people perform to maintain or enhance their well-being. People start by making a choice among food products, then making a purchase, and then consuming the food, which results in nutrient intake. Each step is connected to, but not determined solely by, the previous step. Nutrient intake cannot occur without consumption, except in cases like a program of parenteral infusion during a post-operative period. Consumption is connected to, but not determined solely by, purchase because of factors like food waste and food preparation methods. Purchase is connected to, but not determined solely by, choice because of factors like availability.

These behaviors need to be differentiated for two reasons. First, if these behaviors are caused by unique, independent factors that are the necessary and sufficient determinants, then these behaviors are themselves unique. Two unique, necessary and sufficient causes cannot lead to the same behavior. Second, these behaviors take on different meanings to researchers. For example, epidemiologists may view nutrient intake as the important aspect of food-related behavior, whereas marketers may view purchase as the important aspect of behavior.

Choice Behavior. Choice behavior reflects an individual's decision to purchase or consume a food. This behavior is the individual's *intention* to perform the behavior, where intention is a belief that links the person with some action (such as purchasing or consuming a specific food product).

Choice differs from purchase and consumption behavior in that a person's decision about a food does not necessarily determine purchase or consumption behavior; that is, the determinants of purchase and consumption behavior are not the same as the determinants of choice behavior. In some cases, a person's choice may be determined by his or her attitude toward the product. Suppose that a person decides to purchase oranges based on his or her attitude and goes to the store to implement this decision. At the store, the person discovers that oranges are not available or is exposed to information from point-of-purchase displays. Both these new events may change the original food choice, suggesting that choice and purchase assess different constructs.

When the researcher's focus is on "informed choices," choice behavior is used as a criterion variable. Many nutrition educators have argued that one aim of their work is to provide individuals with information to make informed choices concerning what foods to consume. This information is designed to change individuals' beliefs about foods in order to influence their food choices (i.e., to select foods that will lead to beneficial dietary practices). Nutrition educators have little control over many factors that may affect purchase and consumption behavior (e.g., food availability, food price); consequently, choice behavior is a desirable criterion because it can be affected by education.

Purchase Behavior. Purchase behavior is the acquisition of food by an exchange of money (or a similar resource such as goods or services) for food. Most people in the United States purchase the foods that they consume. Several factors, other than choice, can influence purchase behavior. The situation (context) in which the purchase behavior occurs and the pricing, placement of product, and packaging may affect whether purchases are made.

Purchase behavior has been differentiated from consumption behavior and nutrient intake for several reasons. First, the determinants of purchase are different from the determinants of consumption and nutrient intake. Factors such as food cost, food availability, or habit often affect purchase directly. The effects of these factors on consumption are mediated through the purchase behavior in that these factors affect consumption indirectly by affecting purchase behavior. Second, the purchase of a food does not mean that the food will be consumed. For example, an individual may give the food away as a gift or may prepare it in a way that makes it inedible.

Purchase behavior is used as a criterion variable for several reasons. First, factors that affect purchase behavior directly may be the focus of the research. In some cases, a researcher may be interested in examining the effect of pricing strategy, product packaging, or product placement at the point of purchase on product purchase. Second, purchase behavior may be used as an indicator of economic growth and stability for food producers. Choice, consumption, and nutrient intake measures would not provide an adequate index of expenditure.

Consumption Behavior. Consumption is the actual intake of food. Most of the time, food consumption corresponds closely to nutrient intake, where nutrient intake refers to the nutrients ingested that are available for absorption by the body. The consumption of vitamin and mineral supplements serves as an example of the possible lack of correspondence between food consumption and nutrient intake. Consumption also does not imply that an individual retains the food. For instance, the eating pattern of bulimics will result in limited correspondence between consumption and nutrient intake.

Factors other than choice and purchase affect consumption. An individual may purchase a certain type of food, but not know how the food should be stored. This lack of preservation knowledge may lead to food spoilage and, thus, no consumption. Food acceptability also may affect consumption. An individual may prepare a food, but not consume it because it tastes bad.

A major distinction between food consumption and nutrient intake is at the level of analysis. When food consumption is measured, the nutrient intake of an individual often is estimated by using food composition tables. In some cases, individuals are asked to keep samples of foods that they consume, and the nutrient composition of these foods is analyzed. Thus, consumption differs from nutrient intake in that consumption is a behavior, and nutrient intake is an outcome; that is, a result of the consumption behavior. Nutrient intake does not necessarily reflect the occurrence of any single behavior or set of behaviors. In other words, individuals may have similar nutrient intakes, but display a variety of consumption behaviors.

Consumption behavior is used as the behavioral component of food guides. These guides contain suggestions on the number of servings (to be consumed) from each food grouping. Consumption behavior also is used by the U.S. Department of Agriculture for measuring and appraising trends in dietary practices (Burk and Pao, 1976).

Food, nutrition, and marketing researchers have used measures of food consumption to describe different segments (clusters) in the population. The main focus of this research effort is to segment the population into identifiable groupings, by using behavioral indicants as the descriptor variables, and to relate these market segments to selected external variables (e.g., sociodemographic factors, self-image). For example, Akin, Guilkey, Popkin, and Fanelli (1986) used the 1977-1978 Nationwide Food Consumption Survey to develop and test a segmentation scheme that classified respondents according to consumption patterns. These patterns then were related to sociodemographic factors. In their study, ethnic group membership (i.e., black and white) and residence (i.e., Southern and non-Southern) were the most important factors associated with the market segments. Several other authors (e.g., Baird and Schutz, 1976, 1980; Leonard, 1982; Sadalla and Burroughs, 1983) have used segmentation strategies to identify eating profiles. For example, Leonard (1982) identified five clusters of respondents based on food-consumption practices: Meat Eaters, People on the Go, In a Dither, Conscientious, and Healthy Eater. The use of consumption measures as a means for describing groups of individuals provides some insight into the types of food-related behaviors that characterize market segments. This research approach is limited, however, because factors that determine these behaviors often are not identified.

Nutrient Intake. Nutrient intake refers to the ingestion of nutrients that are available for absorption by the body. Nutrient intake is often used as a proxy for nutritional status and is used to assess potential health risks. Nutritionists often make the assumption that individuals who meet the Recommended Dietary Allowances (or some percent of the RDAs) will be appropriately nourished--that is, nutritional status will be evaluated as "good." Discrepancies between individuals' nutrient intakes and the RDAs may indicate low, excessive, or unbalanced nutrient intakes. In this case, nutritional status will be evaluated as "poor." The assumption that nutrient intake is a good indicator of nutritional status is appropriate in healthy populations, but is not valid for individuals who have some disease that inhibits nutrient absorption and utilization.

A Framework for Organizing the Measurements of Food-Related Behavior

The Framework. A number of measures exist for the assessment of food-related behavior. Brinberg and Jaccard's (1989) framework for integrating measurement procedures is used to organize the measures of food-related behavior. Four facets help to structure measurement procedures and to identify some of their strengths and weaknesses. One facet is the *source of the information*; that is, whether the individual provides the information concerning his or her own food-related behavior or whether an outside observer provides the information. A second facet is *the role of time* in the assessment procedure; that is, whether the measure assesses behaviors that have occurred in the past, in the present, or will occur in the future. A third facet is the *obtrusiveness of the measurement procedure*; that is, the extent to which the procedure affects that which it measures. A fourth facet is the *level of detail* (detailed or cursory) in which the behavior is described; that is, the extent to which the researcher examines an individual's behavior on repeated occasions. Table 2-1 illustrates these four facets which organize the characteristics of different measurement procedures.

The facets used to construct Table 2-1 can be used to describe traditional measures of food-related behavior as well as to suggest alternative measurement procedures. For instance, a 24-hour recall of food consumption is 1) a subject's self-report, 2) concerned with the occurrence of past behaviors, 3) somewhat obtrusive because the respondent is aware that he or she is providing information, and 4) somewhat superficial in its assessment of food consumption. This procedure would be placed in cell 13 of Table 2-1. Another approach

Table 2-1

Facets for Organizing Measures of Food-Related Behavior

		Subject			Observer		
		past	present	future	past	present	future
D E T A I L	obtrusive	1	2	3	4	5	6
	unobtrusive	7	8	9	10	11	12
C U R S O R Y	obtrusive	13	14	15	16	17	18
	unobtrusive	19	20	21	22	23	24

for assessing food-related behavior could be direct observation of an individual's behavior. This assessment procedure 1) uses an outside observer as the source of information, 2) is concurrent with the occurrence of the behaviors, 3) is somewhat obtrusive if the respondent is aware that he or she is being observed, and 4) can provide detailed information, if multiple observations are made. This measurement procedure would be placed in cell 5 of Table 2-1. A third approach for measuring food-related behavior is to use trace measures (e.g., garbage). This measurement procedure 1) uses the subject as the source of the information, 2) measures records of past behavior, 3) is unobtrusive because the measurement procedure does not affect the performance of the behaviors, and the subject is unaware that the information is being collected, and 4) can provide a detailed analysis of the behavior, if multiple observations are made. This procedure would be placed in cell 7 of Table 2-1. A fourth approach would be a 7-day food diary. This procedure 1) uses the subject as the source of the information, 2) is concurrent with the occurrence of the behavior (i.e., the behavior is recorded immediately following its occurrence), 3) is somewhat obtrusive, and 4) provides some detail. This procedure would be placed in cell 2 of Table 2-1. A fifth approach for measuring food-related behavior is to use an experiential sampling procedure (Larson and Csikszentmihalyi, 1983). When using this procedure, the subject would be contacted by the researcher (e.g., by using a "beeper") and asked to list all foods consumed in the past hour. The subject would be contacted on a random basis during the course of the study. This assessment procedure 1) uses the subject as the source of information, 2) is concurrent with the occurrence of the behaviors, 3) is obtrusive because the assessment disrupts the ongoing behavior, and the respondent is aware that he or she is providing information, and 4) provides some detail, if multiple observations are collected across a range of situations. This measurement procedure would be placed in cell 2 of Table 2-1.

By combining different facets found in Table 2-1, novel assessment procedures for examining food-related behavior may be suggested. One assessment procedure not used currently is experiential sampling with an outside observer (e.g., a family member), rather than the individual under study, to assess certain food-related behaviors (cell 11 of Table 2-1). A potential strength of this approach is its relative unobtrusiveness when compared to traditional experiential sampling. An inherent limitation is the lack of coordination between the request for information and the recording of that information; that is, the observer may not be in contact with the subject when the request for information is made.

The researcher also could use an observer (source) to conduct repeated observations (depth) to determine what foods the subject purchases (concurrent) (e.g., observe purchase behavior at the local supermarket). The relationship of the observer to the situation and the subject is likely to affect whether the assessment procedure is obtrusive. If the observer is a natural feature of the situation (e.g., stock clerks at the supermarket), then the assessment is likely to be relatively unobtrusive (cell 11 in Table 2-1). If the observer is not a normal part of the situation (e.g., a researcher with a clipboard in hand), then the procedure is likely to be relatively obtrusive (cell 5 in Table 2-1). Scanner data (i.e., records of purchase behavior recorded at the point of purchase), collected at a single point in time, are an unobtrusive measure of past behavior whose source is the subject (cell 19 in Table 2-1). A shopping list may be used as an indicant of future behavior. This measurement procedure 1) uses the subject as the source of the information, 2) is somewhat obtrusive, if the list is generated at the request of the researcher, 3) is detailed, if the list is for food purchases for the coming week, and 4) is a measure of future behavior. This procedure would be placed in cell 3 of Table 2-1. As a final example, a procedure that uses an observer (source), who casually records a subject's current behavior (depth and time), and is undetected by the subject would be placed in cell 23 of Table 2-1. For instance, an observer interested in food consumption at a fast-food restaurant could sit at this type of restaurant and observe the types of foods people consume.

   Strength and Limitations of Each Facet. Table 2-2 contains a brief summary of some strengths and weaknesses of each level of each facet specified in Table 2-1. Our intent here is to be illustrative, and not exhaustive. The entries presented in Table 2-2 may be found in the discussion of measurement issues in most standard research methods books (e.g., Kerlinger 1973). Each facet in Table 2-1 has several *potential* strengths and *inherent* limitations. The strengths are described as *potential* because the researcher can implement the assessment procedure in a way that reduces (or eliminates) the strength of that procedure. One strength of an unobtrusive measurement is that the naturally occurring behavior is not disrupted. The researcher, however, might inadvertently make his or her presence known; thus, disrupting the behavior. The weaknesses, however, are *inherent*. If the researcher selects a particular assessment procedure, then the limitations associated with that procedure can not be eliminated.

Table 2-2 provides only the briefest summary of subject factors. These factors reflect the subject's biases and memory limitations as well as the interaction between the subject and the instrument. Researchers who have examined and compared traditional measures of food consumption such as 24-hour recall, food frequency, 1-, 3-, or 7-day food records (see Burk and Pao, 1976; and Krantzler *et al.*, 1982) have focused primarily on the effect of subject factors on the quality of the measures.

Dwyer, Krall, and Coleman (1987) describe several consistent findings that emerge from studies that evaluate the validity of retrospective measures: 1) individuals vary in their recall completeness, 2) individuals sometimes recall foods never eaten, and 3) individuals report inaccurate amounts and kinds of foods. These findings reflect issues that affect the manner in which information is recalled from memory. Dwyer *et al.* (1987) argue that memory factors may account for the invalidity of retrospective data. For instance, subjects may be inattentive to the foods that they consume when other aspects of the situation are more salient. This inattentiveness would lead to poor recall because the information (i.e., which foods were eaten) was not encoded into memory. Other memory factors that may influence recall are interference (e.g., memory of former food habits that affect the recall of current food consumption) and belief elaboration (e.g., respondent creates beliefs concerning food consumption not related to actual intake).

Several researchers (e.g., Tversky and Kahneman, 1974) have proposed a set of heuristics that individuals use to recall information from memory. One of these heuristics--availability--is likely to affect recall of food consumption. This heuristic has been defined as a judgment criterion that respondents use when estimating the

Table 2-2

Some Strengths and Weaknesses of Time, Source, Obtrusiveness and Depth

Time-Past	Strength	Provides basis/baseline and historical context for interpreting behavior.
	Weakness	Misrepresentation of past information. Weak linkage between measures and concept.
Time-Present	Strength	Assessment of current behavior.
	Weakness	Little historical/contextual perspective.
Time-Future	Strength	Allows prediction of behavior.
	Weakness	Unknown internal or external changes. Social desirability. Prediction biases.
Source-Subject	Strength	Access to own behavior. Ease of data collection.
	Weakness	Biases in reporting behavior. Inability to access some behaviors. Subject role biases.
Source-Observer	Strength	Less susceptible to attributional bias.
	Weakness	Inability to observe all behaviors; e.g., choice. Deliberate filtering of information.
Obtrusive	Strength	Controlled view of behavior.
	Weakness	Interference with natural unfolding of behaviors.
Unobtrusive	Strength	Allows behaviors to occur without disruption. Access to private information.
	Weakness	No control of timing/patterning of behavior. Constrained view of phenomena.
Depth - Detail	Strength	Rich description, scrutiny of behavior. Careful monitoring of measurement.
	Weakness	Overwhelming amount of information. Difficulty in recognizing general patterns.
Depth - Cursory	Strength	Allows broad perspective of behaviors.
	Weakness	Superficial examination of behaviors. Contextual richness is ignored.

frequency of an event (e.g., the frequency of eating a particular type of food). By using this heuristic, respondents are affected by the ease with which instances come to mind. For example, respondents may find that the consumption of meat comes to mind more easily than a candy bar. Because the availability heuristic leads to a systematic bias in the estimated frequency of the event (i.e., the consumption of meat), meats will be recalled as eaten more frequently than a candy bar, even though both food products may be consumed with equal frequency.

An additional subject-based effect that may influence the validity of food-related behavior measures is the orientation the subject takes toward the instrument. In some cases, the respondents may choose to present themselves in a favorable light by providing socially desirable responses--such as eating fruits and vegetables when these foods are not consumed. An alternative orientation would be more negative; that is, the respondent might deliberately recall food consumption that does not represent accurately food intake. A more detailed discussion of these subject orientations may be found in Webb, Campbell, Schwartz, Sechrest, and Grove (1981).

Both depth and obtrusiveness facets presented in Table 2-2 have received some attention in the literature. The obtrusiveness of the measures have been discussed in the comparison of trace measures (e.g., garbology) and self-reports (e.g., 24-hour recall). The depth of the measures has been discussed in the comparisons of qualitative versus quantitative methods (e.g., Achterberg, 1988). These issues are addressed in more detail in the next section.

Current Measures of Food-Related Behavior

In Table 2-1, four facets for organizing the measurements of food-related behavior were presented. Current researchers have applied methods that represent only some of the cells in this table to the study of food-related behavior. These methods can be organized into three classes of measures: self-report measures, trace measures, and observational measures.

Self-Report Measures. The primary characteristics of self-report measures are 1) the respondent is the source of the information, and 2) the respondent is aware that this information is being recorded. Because these measures for assessing food-related behavior have received the greatest amount of attention (see the review by Krantzler *et al.*, 1982), numerous issues have been raised concerning factors that limit the validity of these measures. Three sets of issues seem to cause the most concern. One issue focuses on whether an interviewer is present and records the information or whether the respondent provides the information in private (or at least not in the presence of the researcher or interviewer). Karkeck (1987) and Burk and Pao (1976) discuss how the interviewer may influence the measurement of food intake. In some cases, respondents may wish to present themselves to the interviewer as having a healthful diet and modify (i.e., not tell the truth about) their report of food consumption.

A second issue focuses on the time the behavior occurred; that is, whether the information is obtained for current food-related behavior or for behavior that has occurred in the past. The method typically used to measure current behavior is food records (diaries), although an experiential sampling approach also would provide similar information. The food record method, however, is susceptible to several possible confounding factors. Some research (e.g., Dennis and Shifflett, 1985) indicates that the act of recording current behavior inhibits spontaneous food selection (e.g., snacks are consumed less frequently during a recording period).

The methods typically used to measure past food-related behavior are 24-hour recalls, food-frequency measures (of either one or six month durations), and dietary histories. A detailed description of each of these methods may be found in Burk and Pao (1976). Factors that bias the findings from these methods were presented in our discussion of the strengths and weaknesses of measures that use the respondent as the source of the information (see Table 2-2).

A third issue is whether aids, models, or lists are used when measures of food-related behavior are obtained. Some biases may occur in the use of these models and measures. One type of aid is measuring cups. Foods that are inconvenient to measure (such as snacks) are less likely to be reported (Burk and Pao, 1976). In addition, respondents may alter their behavior to simplify their recording of food intake. The list-recall method both facilitates and constrains the measure of food-behavior. The method facilitates recall by providing a structure for organizing responses (e.g., by using a cycle of food activity such as a major shopping trip). This method constrains recall because respondents are less likely to report foods that are not part of the major shopping trip.

In spite of the numerous biases associated with self-report methods, this approach for measuring food-related behavior is used extensively. Three factors account for its use--ease of data collection, relatively low cost, and the (presumed) advantage of the respondent's awareness of his or her behavior.

Trace measures. The primary characteristics of trace measures are 1) the respondent is the source of the information, and 2) the respondent is unaware that he or she is providing information. Trace measures of food-related behavior are receiving increased attention because they are not constrained by the same limitations associated with self-report measures (i.e., biases that may be attributed to respondents' awareness that their behavior is being recorded). Rathje (1984) and his associates (e.g., Cote, McCullough, and Reilly, 1985) have examined food consumption by an analysis of garbage (e.g., examining food packages, food waste). Several unexpected findings resulted from these studies using trace measures. Trying new foods led to greater food waste, and the purchase of specialty food items and the hoarding of foods (e.g., during a food shortage) led to greater food loss. These authors hypothesized that the greater loss is associated with limited knowledge of food preservation. These researchers also used trace measures to examine alcohol consumption. Specifically, these authors conducted both interviews and garbage analysis to measure the impact of a new liquor store outlet. The interview data indicated no change in alcohol consumption after the opening of the liquor store. The household refuse, however, revealed an increase in the discard of beer, wine, and liquor containers.

In a seminal analysis of trace measures, Webb, Campbell, Schwartz, Sechrest, and Grove (1981) presented three fundamental (and potential) sources of invalidity that need to be addressed when using trace measures to examine food-related behavior: sampling of measures, categorizing the measures (i.e., a coding system), and linking the measures to the underlying construct (such as food consumption). Trace measures are susceptible to sampling biases similar to those biases associated with self-report measures; that is, the extent to which a measure obtained for a single time period (e.g., 24-hour recall) is representative of the food-related behavior (e.g., consumption). Rathje (1984) presents a sampling strategy (i.e., a random sampling of time periods and locations over a long time period) that reduces the likelihood of sampling bias. A second potential difficulty in the use of trace measures is the manner in which the data are recorded. Because trace measures do not lend themselves to simple quantitative indices, coding systems are needed to organize and structure the array of trace measures. A third potential limitation is the evaluation of the trace measure's ability to represent the underlying construct (such as consumption). One strategy for assessing the construct validity of a trace measure is to collect additional data to triangulate with the findings based on the trace measures. Triangulation is a procedure that allows the researcher to assess the convergence of empirical findings across different methods. For example, trace measures of food packages may be triangulated with self-report measures of food consumption. If these measures converge, then our confidence in both measures as valid indicants of the underlying construct (i.e., consumption) increases. If these measures do not converge, however, then either or both measures may be inadequate.

An emerging technology that may be used as a source of trace measures of food-related behavior is electronic scanner services. Scanner data are used to measure actual purchases (rather than self-reports of purchase behavior) and may be described as a trace measure because the respondent is the source of the information and is typically unaware of the information that he or she is leaving behind. Currently, this form of data is used to provide better inventory control, to improve labor productivity, and to examine a variety of marketing projects such as new product test markets or product repositioning (Dillon, Madden, and Firtle, 1987). Scanner data have been combined with panel data to provide detailed information concerning the relationship between purchase behavior and the demographic characteristics of the panel. Future research efforts that examine food-related behavior should begin to adapt this new technology as one type of behavioral measure.

Direct Observation. The primary characteristics of direct observation are 1) the observer is the source of the information, and 2) the respondent may (or may not) be aware that he or she is providing information. The level of awareness would depend on whether the observer is visible to or hidden from the respondent. Carter, Sharbaugh and Stapell (1981) used observers to record actual food intake of children at scheduled meals. Michela and Contento (1986) used parents (typically mothers) to estimate the food consumption of their child.

Direct observation must be transformed by the use of some type of coding system. Two factors can be used to structure the development of a coding system--unit of analysis and single vs. multiple codes. The unit of analysis may be viewed as a continuum of micro-level to macro-level analysis. A macro-level unit contains numerous components, whereas the micro-level unit represents the "basic building blocks." For example, the specific food that an individual consumes (e.g., apple) may be viewed as a micro-level unit, whereas food groups (e.g., fruit) may be viewed as a macro-level unit.

A second factor is whether the codes in the observational system are treated as mutually exclusive and exhaustive or whether multiple coding of food is allowed. Suppose that an individual eats a sandwich that contains turkey, roast beef, lettuce, tomatoes, and mustard. This food might receive a single code (e.g., a deli sandwich) or receive multiple codes (e.g., meat, garnish, and condiments). A strength of the former approach is its ability to organize the foods into "neat" and definable segments. The strength of the latter approach is its ability to allow multiple codes for each food consumed. The weakness, however, is the increased complexity in the analysis and interpretation of the multiple codes.

There are several possible sources of invalidity with the use of observational methods. One possible source is the constraints imposed by the coding system. Although a coding system structures observations, it also constrains what the observer can record; that is, the observer is trained to ignore all those events that are not contained in the coding system. For example, suppose that an observer was trained to use a coding system that only examined foods from the four food groups. Because candy bars and alcoholic beverages are not traditionally considered as part of the four food groups, consumption of these products would not be coded by the observer, even though these products had been consumed by the individual. A second possible source of invalidity is the adequacy of the sample selected for observation. This limitation is similar to the representativeness problems of self-reports and trace measures. That is, the quality of the information collected by using self-report and trace measures is constrained by the periods from which the measures are selected. For instance, the quality of self-report measures of food consumption (e.g., a 24-hour recall) is affected by which days are selected. A third possible source of invalidity is that the observer may not have access to some types of information (e.g., food-related attitudes). This lack of information may result in incomplete data. A fourth possible source of invalidity is the biases that the observer brings to the situation. One mechanism for addressing this limitation, however, is the use of multiple judges and the assessment of inter-judge reliability.

Because of the resources (both time and labor) involved in the development of a coding scheme, the sampling of the behaviors, and the collection and analysis of this form of data, few researchers have used this approach to measure food-related behavior. Its strengths, however, offer researchers an opportunity to collect data that are not susceptible to the same biases as those for self-report and trace measures.

Criteria for Evaluating the Measurement of Food-Related Behavior

Numerous validation studies have been conducted to compare different measures of food-related behavior. The article by Krantzler *et al.* (1982) contains abstracts of 87 articles that focus on either the evaluation of a single measure of food-related behavior or the comparison of various measures. Since 1982, dozens of additional articles have appeared in the literature that evaluate and compare measures of food-related behavior. Although a systematic integration of these research findings is needed, the focus in this section is to provide a framework for evaluating food-related behavior measures and not to present a comprehensive review of the literature.

Two research strategies characterize the evaluation of measures of food-related behavior. One strategy involves the evaluation and comparison of various measures of food-related behavior. This strategy contains two distinct approaches. In one approach, researchers compare alternative measures of food-related behavior (e.g., 24-hour recall versus 3-day diary) in which the respondent reports his or her food consumption. By using this approach, researchers can not determine the "validity" of any one method. In the second approach, researchers compare a self-report measure with an "objective assessment"; that is, a method in which the experimenter measures food consumption by weighing and recording food prior to consumption and then records food waste after consumption. By using this approach, the researcher is able to determine whether deviations occur between the self-report measure and an external, "correct" standard.

The second research strategy involves the evaluation of a measure of food-related behavior either within an individual or across individuals.   One aspect of this research compares intraindividual versus interindividual variability indices of food-related behavior. For example, Hunt, Leonard, Garry, and Goodwin (1983) compared different indices of variability and found that intraindividual variability was consistently greater than interindividual variability. These indices of variability are assessed most often with respect to food nutrients. One important implication of these findings is that intraindividual variability may mask the effect of education interventions that examine dietary changes across groups.   That is, intraindividual variability affects the power of a study to detect differences across various treatment groups.

The variety of facets used to evaluate and contrast measures of food-related behavior has been substantial.   For example, numerous populations, cultures, foods, nutrients, institutional settings, time periods, and interventions have been used for evaluating measures of food-related behavior. These facets may be divided into two general categories--methodological and substantive facets. The methodological facets--time, depth, source, and obtrusiveness-- were presented in Table 2-1 and provide a structure for examining the measures of food-related behavior.   Brinberg and McGrath (1985) and Brinberg and Jaccard (1986) present a set of facets for organizing a substantive area such as food-related behavior of individuals. This set of facets includes actors, behaviors and context. The first facet-- actors--refers to those characteristics that the individual brings to the study that may influence his or her food-related behavior. Two broad categories help to structure these characteristics--sociodemographic and psychological. The first category includes variables such as age, education, gender, income, race, or religion. The second category includes variables such as beliefs, attitudes, personality traits, values, needs, and emotions. Researchers have focused on variables in the sociodemographic category to evaluate and compare the effectiveness of measures across these different variables. Bazzarre, Yuhas, and Wu (1983) compared 3-day records, diet histories, and 24-hour recalls for elderly respondents. Hunt *et al.* (1983) also examined elderly respondents, but focused on evaluating the use of dietary records. Klesges, Klesges, Brown, and Frank (1987) evaluated the 24-hour recall measure by examining the dietary practices of children. Some researchers (e.g., Basiotis, Welsh, Cronin, Kelsay, and Mertz, 1987) have examined the differences in the responses of men and women to traditional measures of food consumption. Gersovitz, Madden, and Smiciklas-Wright (1978) compared 24-hour recalls and 7-day records for respondents with little education (a mean of 9th grade) and limited income (mean of $3,270). The psychological factors (e.g., attitudes, values) have not received much attention when researchers have compared measures of food-related behaviors.

The second facet--behavior--refers to food-related behaviors. Typically, researchers have focused on food consumption, although food choice, food purchases, and nutrient intake have been examined. Future research is needed to examine how the measurement of these different food-related behaviors vary across actors and contexts. The third facet--context--includes factors such as culture, food at home or away from home, and institutionalized respondents. Hankin, Rhoads and Glober (1975) compared 1-day and 7-day food recalls by using Japanese respondents, and Heady (1961) evaluated a 7-day food record by using British respondents. Similar comparisons of the traditional measures of food consumption have examined Hawaiian men (e.g., McGee, Rhoads, Hankin, Yano, and Tillotson, 1982).

As is evident from this brief description of facets, measures of food-related behavior have received substantial attention. Unfortunately, these research efforts have not been systematic in their evaluation and comparison of measures of food intake. This aimless approach toward the evaluation of measures of food-related behavior does not provide researchers with the knowledge to determine the conditions under which specific measures of food-related behavior will be effective. That is, the researcher cannot determine the effect of factors such as actor characteristics, the types of food-related behavior, and context on the effectiveness of any specific measure of food-related behavior.

Multitrait-Multimethod Approach. The multitrait-multimethod (MTMM) approach (Campbell and Fiske, 1959) provides a useful framework for developing research strategies to evaluate the validity of various measures of food-related behavior. Briefly, the MTMM approach assesses four features of "methods" and "traits." "Methods" and "traits" have been placed in quotes to indicate that a number of variables may be considered a method in one case and a trait in another. These four features are illustrated by the following questions. First, does one "method" measuring the same "trait" result in consistent findings? This finding is referred to as the **reliability** of the "method." Second, do different "methods" measuring the same "trait" lead to consistent findings? This finding is referred to as **convergent validity**. Third, does the same "method" used to assess different "traits" result in different findings? This finding is referred to as "**method variance**." Fourth, do different "methods" used to measure different "traits" result in different findings? This finding (in conjunction with the finding from the third feature) is referred to as **discriminant validity**.

When using the MTMM approach, a researcher creates a correlation matrix of the "method-trait" pairings. These correlations are used to determine reliability, convergent, and discriminant validity. The hypothesized outcome when using the MTMM approach is that 1) the reliability coefficients will be significantly greater than zero (and, ideally, not significantly different from 1.0); 2) the convergent validity coefficients will be significantly greater than zero (and, ideally, not significantly different from 1.0 or significantly different from the reliability coefficients), and 3) the method variance and discriminant validity coefficients will not be significantly different from zero and will be significantly different from the reliability and convergent validity coefficients.

A traditional application of the MTMM approach would be to use various measures of food-related behavior (e.g., 24-hour recall, 7-day food diary) as the methods and the food groups as the traits. For these methods and traits, the MTMM approach allows the researcher to assess the reliability, convergent, and discriminant validity of the various methods to assess food consumption with respect to various food groups. Suppose that each individual in the study was asked to provide several (e.g., five) nonconsecutive, 24-hour recalls and also was asked to maintain several 7-day food diaries (e.g., on 5 separate occasions several months apart). For each individual in the study, the researcher would be able to estimate the reliability of each method for each food group, the convergence of the methods for each food group, and the discriminant validity of the methods.

The MTMM approach also may be used to examine the reliability, convergence, and discrimination of other variables. Suppose that a researcher is interested in using observers to examine the purchase behavior of dairy products for men and women. Assume that dairy product purchases by men and women are uncorrelated; i.e., the types of dairy products purchased by men are unrelated to the types of dairy products purchased by women. The different observers are treated as the methods and males and females are treated as the traits. This use of the MTMM approach would provide the following information. First, the consistency of each observer (method) concerning his or her observations of the dairy purchase behavior of each gender (trait) is assessed; that is, the reliability of the observer. Second, the convergent validity of the methods (observers) is assessed; that is, whether different observers (method) of the same gender (trait) record consistent observations. Third, the method variance associated with the method (observer) is determined; that is, whether the same observer (method) who views the purchase behavior of the different traits (men or women) records different observations. Fourth, the discriminant validity of the methods (observers) is established; that is, whether different methods (observers) measuring different traits (men or women) result in distinct findings.

One additional example may help to illustrate the flexibility of the MTMM approach. Suppose that respondents are treated as methods and settings--food at home and food away from home--are treated as traits. Several nonconsecutive, 24-hour recall measures could be obtained for the respondent-setting pairing. This configuration of the MTMM does provide information concerning the consistency of each respondent's behavior (i.e., food consumption) at a setting (e.g., food at home), the similarity across respondents' behavior for one setting (e.g., food at home), the similarity (or differences) of each respondent's behavior at different settings (e.g., food at home or food away from home), and the similarity (or differences) of the behavior of different respondents at different settings.

Generalizability Theory. The dominant approach used to assess reliability has been classic test theory (e.g., Nunnally, 1978). Briefly, this theory asserts that any measure (X) is determined by two factors: a true score and a random error component. Three stated assumptions are associated with this theory: 1) the mean of the error scores is zero, 2) the correlation between the true score and the error score is zero, and 3) the correlation between the error scores of two variables is zero. One major assumption underlies this theory--that error is an unidimensional, undifferentiated concept. That is, classic test theory does not differentiate among different sources or types of errors.

Cronbach and his associates (1963, 1972) have developed an approach that combines reliability and validity issues into a single framework--generalizability theory. This theory was developed, in part, because of the strong assumption underlying classic test theory; that is, a single error component. According to generalizability theory, "an interest in the 'reliability' of a given measure is based on a desire to *generalize* from the observation involved to some other class of observations" (Wiggins, 1973, pg 285). From a generalizability perspective, a researcher concerned with interobserver reliability (e.g., two or more observers who record the dietary practices of people at a restaurant) would focus on whether a given set of observations (made by one set of observers) would generalize to those observations that other observers might make.

An important feature of generalizability theory is its ability to analyze the variance components that contribute to measurement error by using analysis of variance techniques to evaluate the impact of these various sources of error. The measurement of food-related behavior may be affected by several sources of error. One potential source of error is the characteristics of the person who provides the information. For example, systematic differences may exist in the measurement of food-related behavior for children, adolescents, and adults. The age of the respondent, then, may be treated as one potential source of error variance. A second potential source of error is the amount of time used to measure food-related behavior (e.g., 24-hour recall, 3-day diary, 7-day diary). A 24-hour recall and a 7-day diary may differ significantly in estimating fiber intake. The main issue underlying this stream of research is the representativeness of measures for assessing nutrient intake.

The strength of applying generalizability theory, rather than an analysis of separate factors that affect the measurement of food-related behavior, is that its use makes the researcher more aware of the need to consider multiple sources of error and the possible interaction among these sources of error. For instance, by using the age of the respondent and the amount of time as two factors in a generalizability study, the researcher is able to assess the interaction (in an analysis of variance sense) between these two factors. One type of interaction could be as follows: Suppose that a 24-hour recall estimates a low level of fiber intake for adolescents, whereas a 3-day diary estimates a higher level of daily fiber intake. Further suppose that a 24-hour recall estimates a high level of fiber intake for adults, whereas a 3-day diary estimates a lower level of daily fiber intake. This interaction between the age of the respondent and the amount of time for estimating fiber intake would not be detected with traditional studies; that is, the analysis of these factors independently. Thus, generalizability theory serves as a powerful tool for evaluating the variety of factors that affect the measures of food-related behavior.

The material presented in this chapter makes apparent that food-related behavior has been measured in a variety of ways. Because all measures are fallible and constrained by different limitations, the use of multiple methods enables the researcher to evaluate the effect of measurement types on empirical findings. Self-report measures of food consumption are constrained by respondent biases (both memory and recall biases). Trace measures are not constrained by these biases, but are affected by other factors (e.g., sampling, linking the measure to the construct). The use of both methods, however, allows the researcher to triangulate the empirical findings. If multiple methods lead to similar conclusions, then the researcher should have more confidence in the findings because methods with different sources of error are used and result in the same finding. Two assumptions underlie the use of multiple methods: 1) the independent measures can assess the same underlying construct (e.g., food consumption), and 2) the sources of error for the different methods are independent. Numerous researchers in the social sciences (e.g., Brinberg and McGrath, 1985; Webb *et al.*, 1981) and in food and nutrition (e.g., Dennis and Shifflett, 1985) have argued for the use of multiple methods.

3

Food- and nutrition-related attitudes and beliefs are measured because investigators hypothesize that 1) people, in some meaningful way, will differ in their attitudes and beliefs as well as differ in the strength with which their attitudes and beliefs are held, and 2) people who hold different attitudes and beliefs will behave in different ways; that is, these concepts should be determinants of behavior. Attitudes and beliefs are referred to by a number of names like opinions, interests, social determinants, and knowledge in the scientific literature. The first section of this chapter attempts to define the terms beliefs, knowledge, and attitudes. In the second section, some issues related to the measurement of these concepts are examined. Lastly, the relationships among beliefs, knowledge, attitudes, and behavior are explored.

Definitions

According to Fishbein and Ajzen (1975), **beliefs** represent the information that a person has about an object. Conceptually then, beliefs come under the heading of cognition, where cognition is defined as a person's "knowledge, opinions, beliefs, and thoughts about the object" (Fishbein and Ajzen, 1975, pg 12). Fishbein and Ajzen go on to say that "a belief links an object to some attribute," where an object "may be a person, a group of people, an institution, a behavior, a policy, an event, etc.," and the attribute "may be any object, trait, property, quality, characteristic, outcome, or event." Thus, a belief statement contains an object and an associated attribute. One example of a belief statement which illustrates this object-attribute association would be "Breast feeding is convenient," where breast feeding is the object and convenient is the attribute. Another example of a belief statement is "Breast feeding provides the best nutrition," where breast feeding is the object and best nutrition is the attribute.

Once investigators have a belief statement, they need to ascertain an individual's response to that statement. The scale presented most frequently to individuals is a bipolar, adjective scale anchored with agree and disagree. These individuals are asked to state whether they agree or disagree that some object (e.g., breast feeding) is associated with some attribute (e.g., convenient). Another way to measure the perceived association between the object and attribute is to use a subjective probability scale such as likely/unlikely (Fishbein and Ajzen, 1975). Instead of asking whether a person agrees or disagrees that "breast feeding is convenient," the investigator asks a person to indicate how likely or unlikely that "breast feeding is convenient." The subjective probability scale addresses directly the probability that the object and attribute are associated, whereas the investigator must make an inference about the perceived probability when using the agree/disagree response.

In contrast to a belief, which refers to the information that a person has about an object, **attitude** "refers to a person's feelings toward and evaluation of some object, person, issue, or event" (Fishbein and Ajzen, 1975, pg 12). Based on this definition, the distinguishing feature of an attitude is its affective or evaluative component. An example of an attitude statement would be "A high-fiber diet is beneficial." This attitude statement looks deceivingly like a belief statement in that it links an object (A high-fiber diet) with an attribute (beneficial), but this statement becomes an attitude statement by using an evaluative term like beneficial as the attribute.

Generally, attitude measurements have taken two forms. One type often found in the food and nutrition literature takes this form: a statement of affect like "A high-fiber diet is beneficial" is presented, and the individual responds on an agree/disagree scale. The other form is the presentation of a statement or word, and the individual is asked to respond to it on a bipolar, semantic differential scale anchored with evaluative words or statements like good/bad, favorable/unfavorable, like/dislike, beneficial/harmful, and nice/awful. Examples of this form would be a statement like "A high-fiber diet is ..." with a response given on a beneficial/harmful scale or a statement like "Breast feeding my baby would be ..." with a response given on a good/bad scale.

The preceding definitions of beliefs and attitudes reflect the expectancy-value model of attitudes. This model views attitude as an evaluation of some object or act. A person's attitude is determined by two components--a belief (expectancy) and the evaluation (value) of the attribute associated with the belief. These two components are combined by using a multiplicative integration rule (i.e., multiplying the response to a question assessing a belief by the response assessing the evaluation of that belief). The products for each of the beliefs then are summed.

In addition to thinking (having beliefs) and feeling (having attitudes), people behave. **Conation**, according to Fishbein and Ajzen (1975, pg 12), refers to a person's "behavioral intentions and his actions with respect to or in the presence of the object." This definition includes both a person's statement about his or her intention to perform a behavior and a person's actual behavior. Fishbein and Ajzen (1975, pg 12) believe that behavioral intention can be seen as a special case of beliefs, where the person is the object and the intended behavior is the attribute. An example of a behavioral intention statement would be "I plan to breast feed my infant," where the object is I and the behavioral attribute is breast feed. The possible responses to conative statements are the same as the possible responses to statements of beliefs.

Attitudes also have been conceptualized as being composed of three components--affect, cognition, and behavior (Zimbardo, Ebbesen, and Maslach, 1977). This tripartite definition makes attitude a more inclusive concept, that includes verbal statements of affect, of belief, and of behavior. The first component, affect, refers to the individual's overall feelings/emotions toward the attitude object. This component includes both the cognitive evaluation and the emotional "gut-level" reaction to the attitude object. The second component, cognition, is the belief component of the attitude construct. Within the tripartite view, beliefs take on the same meaning as defined previously; that is, beliefs are the perceived link between some object and attribute. The third component, conation (behavior), includes both a person's statement about his or her intention to perform a behavior and a person's actual behavior.

There are several differences between the tripartite view and the expectancy-value view of attitudes. One difference is the separation of affect and cognition in the tripartite view and the inclusion of both affect and cognition as part of the overall evaluation in the expectancy-value view. For instance, an individual may consume a particular food (e.g., spinach) because he believes it is healthy for him (positive cognition), even though he has a negative affective response toward that food (e.g., he becomes somewhat nauseated when eating the food). This example suggests that the separation of affect and cognition is meaningful. An expectancy-value theorist (e.g., Fishbein and Ajzen, 1975), however, would argue that the individual's overall evaluation of the food (i.e., his or her attitude) would capture these conflicting thoughts and feelings. A second difference between these two views is the relationship between conation and cognition. From a tripartite perspective, these constructs are separate concepts and each contributes independently toward the person's attitude. From an expectancy-value perspective, conation is a special case of cognition, where the person is the object and intended behavior is the attribute. When the behavioral belief statement is measured on a subjective probability scale of likely/unlikely, the response indicates how likely a person thinks that he or she will perform a certain behavior. An example of a behavioral intention statement would be "I plan to breast feed my infant," where the object is I and behavioral attribute is breast feed.

The conceptualization of attitudes from a tripartite view has several disadvantages. First, the tripartite definition requires the measurement of beliefs and behavior as well as affect, but it does not give any rules for combining the three measurements into one overall measurement of attitudes. Second, researchers using the tripartite definition have not developed a generally accepted measurement of affect. Third, researchers have not established an independent measure of attitude apart from the tripartite perspective; consequently, the (predictive) validity of the three components cannot be assessed.

Beliefs and attitudes have been presented somewhat differently in the food- and nutrition literature. For example, Sims (1981) offers her definitions of beliefs and attitudes and gives examples of each term. This passage is presented to illustrate how different investigators can use the same words to define concepts, but can draw different conclusions about the concepts' meanings and applications. Sims (1981, pg 463) says that

> "It is possible to distinguish operationally between attitude and belief... The continuum is labeled with "affect" on one end, and "facts" or "cognitions" on the other. If we were to indicate where the entities of attitude and belief would lie upon this continuum, attitudes would be placed toward the affect side, while the belief concept would lie much closer to the fact or cognition set. In other words, those responses or evaluations which cannot be judged as correct or incorrect but are simply based upon an individual's evaluations or feelings toward the object would be labeled attitude. Where beliefs are involved, there should be a distinction between rightness-wrongness, correctness-incorrectness, probable-improbable. Some examples might serve to clarify these concepts: for example, "I eat only the foods that I consider to be healthful for me" would be considered an attitude.

There is no way that this could be judged in terms of correctness or incorrectness. "It is important that all persons eat a diet containing 10 percent animal fat," however would be labeled a belief statement because some empirical evidence indicates that this statement might be more or less correct for certain groups of individuals in the population."

At the beginning of this passage, Sims uses the terms beliefs and attitudes in a manner similar to Fishbein and Ajzen in that attitude lies in the affective domain and belief lies in the cognitive domain. Sims, however, goes on to say that only those statements which can be "judged as correct or incorrect" can be defined as beliefs and that the other statements should be placed in the affective domain. This point represents a departure from Fishbein and Ajzen's definitions of these terms. Specifically, Sims defines attitudes and beliefs from the perspective of the researcher, and Fishbein and Ajzen define them from the perspective of the respondent. That is, Sims says that a statement can be considered a belief only when it can be verified by the researcher, whereas Fishbein and Ajzen's view is that the correctness, likelihood, or probability of a statement is made solely by the respondent.

From the discussion in the preceding paragraph as well as from Sims's passage, a concept seems to be embedded in the cognitive domain, which up to this point has not be articulated. This concept is knowledge. Conceptually, **knowledge** can be defined as those beliefs which are perceived by most people in a community (e.g., a community of nutritionists) as having an object-attribute association with a high probability. In other words, knowledge can be seen as a community's set of strongly-held, widely-accepted beliefs. Thus, there is really no substantial difference between knowledge and beliefs on a conceptual level. There is, however, a difference between knowledge and beliefs on an operational (measurement) level. To illustrate this point, let's take Sims's example of a belief statement "It is important that all persons eat a diet containing 10 percent animal fat." This statement, for the most part, comes under the cognitive domain because it is an object (all persons) linked to an attribute (eat a diet containing 10 percent animal fat). This statement is a measure of belief if the respondents judge it on some agree/disagree or likely/unlikely scale. This statement becomes a measure of knowledge when the individuals' responses to the belief statement are judged correct or incorrect by the researcher using some standard (i.e., the widely-held beliefs of the community to which the research belongs). A test which measures someone's knowledge is simply an evaluation of the fit between two sets of beliefs--the respondents and the test givers.

A final point needs to be made concerning Sims's example of a belief statement. The beginning of the statement starts with "It is important," giving the statement an evaluative or affective tone, even though the second part of the statement clearly falls under the cognitive domain. Consequently, this statement taken in its entirety is difficult to place in either the affective or cognitive domains.

Examples of items used by Guthrie (1988) to study the psychosocial determinants of dietary-fiber consumption serve as a good illustration of the preceding definitions of knowledge, beliefs, and attitudes. Using Ajzen and Fishbein's (1980) definitions (an expectancy-value model), she constructed questionnaire items to measure the attitudes and beliefs associated with the consumption of fiber-rich foods. An example of a belief item was "Eating fresh fruit means I would be eating foods that are high in fiber." The respondents were asked to rate the statement on a 7-point, subjective probability scale ranging from very likely to very unlikely. This questionnaire item conforms to the definition of belief because the respondents were asked their perception of the association between an object (fruit) and an attribute (high in fiber). The evaluation of this belief was measured by asking the respondents to answer the questionnaire item "Eating foods that are high in fiber is ..." on a 7-point, bipolar semantic differential scale anchored with the terms very important to very unimportant. (In this study, the important/

unimportant scale was used to measure evaluation rather than a good/bad scale.) This item conforms to the definition of the evaluation of the belief because the respondents were asked their feelings about the attribute associated with the belief. Guthrie (1988) examined the beliefs toward fruits (in addition to other foods) on six attributes (e.g., not fattening, tastes good). She included an additional item on her questionnaire to obtain an overall measure of attitude towards fruits: "Eating fresh fruit regularly is..." very good/very bad (7-point scale). Examining one person's (e.g., Sue's) answers to this series of questions might indicate that 1) she believes that it is only somewhat likely that fruit is high in fiber (Note: an assessment of her knowledge could be made by checking her answer to a professional's answer), 2) she feels that eating foods that are high in fiber is very important, and 3) she feels that eating fresh fruit regularly is bad. The investigator then can say that Sue feels that eating foods that are high in fiber is very important (evaluation of belief); however, she believes fruits to be only somewhat high in fiber (belief). In addition, Sue considers eating fresh fruit regularly to be a bad experience (attitude). Sue's answers to these questions indicate that beliefs, the evaluation of beliefs, and attitudes do not measure identical underlying constructs.

Measuring Knowledge and Beliefs

Nutrition-related knowledge, beliefs, and attitudes are measured often by investigators for several reasons. First, investigators often explore individuals' level of understanding of nutrition-related concepts in order to develop appropriate nutrition education materials for them. Second, some investigators measure these nutrition-related concepts because they want to determine whether people with a greater understanding of nutrition have better diets. In this section, some measurement issues associated with assessing knowledge and beliefs are discussed. Because the difference between knowledge and beliefs is operational and not conceptual, nutrition knowledge is used as the focal point for the sake of simplicity, but the validity and reliability issues apply equally to beliefs.

A single-measures approach to measuring knowledge is probably the simplest method conceptually. This approach might be called more appropriately the opinion poll approach. Investigators using this approach simply ask individuals to respond to one or more statements or questions like "Breakfast is the most important meal of the day," or "Is orange juice a good source of vitamin C ?" The key feature of this approach is that investigators use each questionnaire item as a variable in subsequent analyses, meaning that the respondents' answers are reported item by item. The assumption underlying this approach is that one item can assess adequately the concept under study.

Most nutrition knowledge measuring instruments, however, are composed of a series of multiple-choice or true-false questions which the respondents are asked to answer. Answers to each item are scored for correctness and then combined in a linear model (i.e., summed). These scores are used to represent the respondents' nutrition knowledge. Several assumptions underlie the development of a single knowledge score or index. One assumption is that these nutrition knowledge tests are valid in that these scores represent real differences (can discriminate) among individuals. In other words, a person with a higher score really does possess greater knowledge than a person with a lower score. A second assumption is that the items used to measure knowledge are unidimensional--that is, the single score derived to represent knowledge assesses a single underlying construct. A third assumption is that these scores are reliable--that is, the same results would be obtained if the test was taken again by the respondents.

Validity. The issues related to the measurement of nutrition knowledge are the same as those related to the construction of any all-purpose achievement test. Nunnally (1978) explains that there are three validity issues--content, construct, and predictive--related to test construction. **Content validity** depends "primarily on the adequacy with which a specified domain of content is sampled" (Nunnally, 1978, pg 91). In other words, content validity is concerned with whether the set of items used to measure the concept is representative of the universe of items for that concept. To illustrate this problem, let's say that the universe of nutrition knowledge relevant to a study is all the information contained in an introductory nutrition textbook. The appropriate question to ask when assessing the content validity of the nutrition knowledge test instrument would be, are the items contained in the instrument representative of all the possible items? Researchers, for the most part, have ignored the problems related to content validity, or at least, they rarely have given any information in their research reports that indicate that they have taken any steps to establish content validity. A simple technique for achieving a representative sample of nutrition knowledge items is to take a number of well-accepted introductory nutrition textbooks and randomly sample information. From this information, specific items can be constructed.

Whereas content validity is concerned with how well the test items reflect the subject being examined, **construct validity** addresses the issue of whether the measurement instrument adequately represents the construct (in this case nutrition knowledge) under study. There is, however, no single strategy for determining the construct validity of a knowledge test. One strategy for assessing construct validity is to compare one test of nutrition knowledge to other tests. If the tests are measuring the same construct (or concept), the results should be similar in that individuals should be rated in a similar manner by all tests. Researchers also have referred to this approach as assessing convergent validity.

Another approach is to examine the relationship of the construct (nutrition knowledge) to another construct (e.g., food intake) which is hypothesized to be predicted by it. Figure 3.1 contains an illustration of the relationships among the constructs and their measures.

Suppose that a researcher believes that nutrition knowledge is related to food consumption--more specifically, greater knowledge

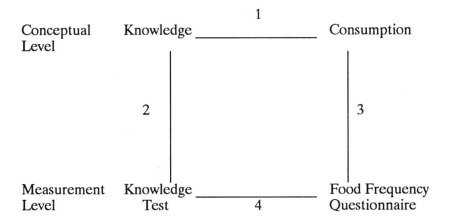

Fig. 3.1.   Illustration of the Construct Validity of a Nutrition Knowledge Test

will be related to higher consumption of dietary fiber and lower consumption of fat. In this case, the researcher assumes that the link (#1) between the concept of knowledge and consumption is true. To assess the construct validity of the measurement of nutrition knowledge (link #2), the researcher also will need to assume that the measure of food consumption is accurate (link #3). The researcher using this strategy for construct validation will collect data about nutrition knowledge (by using a knowledge test) and information about consumption (by using a food-frequency questionnaire) and examine the relationship between the two (link #4). To assess construct validity, the researcher needs to assume two (#1 and #3) of the four links are true, needs to obtain data on one link (#4), and make an inference about the remaining link (#2). To the extent that any of these assumptions are invalid limits the researcher's ability to make an assessment of the construct validity of a measure like nutrition knowledge. As an aside, if the researcher was interested in assessing the construct validity of the consumption measure, he or she would need to assume that the measure of knowledge was an accurate representation of the knowledge concept and that the link between the knowledge and consumption concepts was true. Most often, however, researchers are concerned with making an inference concerning the relationship between the concepts (link #1). To accomplish this task, the researcher needs to assume that the measures accurately represent the concepts (links #2 and #3). The assessment of construct validity using this approach also has been described by some researchers as predictive validity.

Dimensionality. Most researchers of food-related behavior have treated nutrition knowledge as a unidimensional concept. Moxley and Wimberly (1982), however, questioned whether nutrition knowledge is one-dimensional. They (1982, pg 42) succinctly state

> "Is this knowledge monolithic--uniformly responding to the same forces and then contributing to the same dependent effects in a unitary fashion--or is it multi-dimensional? If nutrition knowledge is multidimensional, certain dimensions of nutrition knowledge may differentially influence eating behaviors or other food-related attitudes. Subsequently, causal analyses of nutrition knowledge and behavior, educational programs, and efforts to change food attitudes or eating behaviors should be enhanced by giving special attention to each relevant dimension of knowledge that may affect such attitudes and behaviors."

These investigators (Moxley and Wimberly, 1982) explored the dimensionality of nutrition knowledge by taking 10 food and nutrition knowledge items from a nutrition knowledge instrument designed for children and used by previous investigators. After some revisions, they then had 12 nutritionists determine the answers to the questions. One item was eliminated because of lack of agreement among the professionals as to the correct answer. The 9-item nutrition knowledge test then was administered to 206 nine-year-old children. These authors used factor analytic procedures to examine the relationships among the items in the knowledge test. Factor analysis is a statistical technique that can be used to reduce a larger number of variables into a smaller (but still meaningful) set of variables.

Moxley and Wimberly (1982) found that nutrition knowledge as measured by this instrument was two-dimensional. One dimension (that they labeled "differentiated eating") was composed of items that related to eating behavior; for example, about the importance of eating breakfast every day, and what you eat when you are young will make a difference in your health when you grow up. The second dimension (that they labeled "vitamin importance") was composed of items that were related to whether vitamins are necessary to health. Lastly, these dimensions were only weakly related to each other, meaning children that scored high on the items of one dimension did not necessarily score high on the items of the second dimension. The authors concluded that nutrition knowledge should not be considered a one-dimensional concept.

Reliability. Reliability of a measurement addresses its consistency, stability, and equivalence (with other measures). Consistency refers to the similarity among the items in an instrument and assesses the reliability of a scale for representing the underlying construct (e.g., the consistency among the items in a knowledge test). This form of reliability is typically estimated by either the use of Cronbach's alpha or of part-whole correlations (i.e., the correlation of a specific test item with the total score). For example, if the concept (nutrition knowledge) is unidimensional, then Cronbach's alpha may be calculated to determine the underlying consistency among the test items. Stability refers to the similarity of a response over time and is typically estimated by using a test-retest format (e.g., repeating the same item in an instrument or repeating the instrument on two separate occasions). Equivalence refers to the similarity of responses across alternate forms of the measuring instrument (e.g., two versions of a test to assess nutrition knowledge). Surprisingly, little information concerning the reliability of the measurement of knowledge (or beliefs) is reported in the literature.

Several strategies exist for increasing reliability. Psychometricians (e.g., Nunnally, 1978) have recommended several approaches for increasing the reliability of a respondent's use of an instrument. One approach is to increase the number of items that represent the underlying construct in the instrument. The Spearman-Brown formula (see Nunnally, 1978) is used to estimate the effect of increasing test length on the reliability of the test. By using this formula, the researcher can specify the desired level of reliability and then estimate the number of items to be included in the instrument. A second approach for increasing reliability is to use practice items to allow the respondent to adjust to the particular type of scale used in the instrument. For example, if a researcher measures beliefs by using a 7-point likely/unlikely scale, then several practice items should be administered to the respondent to reduce "warm-up" effects.

A third approach for increasing reliability is to expose the respondent to the range of items (stimuli) to be presented. This approach allows the respondent to establish his or her own standards for responding to the items. A substantial body of research in psychology has illustrated the effect of not exposing the respondent to the range of stimuli. This research (described in the literature as response language issues) has examined the relationship between the individual's perception and his or her response to a rating scale. Individuals may use several strategies for making a response. One prominent strategy is to use the center of the rating scale to correspond with the average subjective value that the individual will judge. Thus, individuals who expect to rate items with high values will generally make lower ratings than individuals who expect to rate items with low values, *even though both individuals have the same perception of the item.* For instance, let's assume that desserts are perceived as more sweet than fruit. Suppose that an individual was asked to rate foods in terms of sweetness and expected to rate desserts (e.g., candy, cookies, ice cream). Now, suppose another individual also was asked to rate foods in terms of sweetness and expected to rate fruits (e.g., strawberries, peaches, and apples). The first individual is likely to rate a particular food (e.g., ice cream) as less sweet than the second individual because the former individual uses the midpoint of the scale to represent sweetness values that are higher, on the average, than the sweetness values expected by the latter individual. As stated previously, response language confounds can be reduced by exposing the respondent to the range of stimuli prior to their rating these stimuli.

A fourth approach for increasing reliability is to eliminate ambiguity in the wording of the questions. For example, a response (e.g., disagreement) to the statement "I serve hamburgers or hot dogs once a week" is ambiguous because 1) you do not know whether the person is responding to the hamburger or to the hot dog portion of the question, and 2) a respondent who serves these items more (or less) than once a week will respond in the same manner--both should disagree with this statement.

One final, but important, issue related to test construction is the application of the criterion of parsimony. Parsimony is defined as "economy in the use of a means to an end" (Webster, 1979). In science, the term is used to mean it is best to use the fewest concepts possible to explain a phenomenon, all other things being equal. As stated previously, nutrition knowledge is a concept that researchers examine because they believe that it will be useful in explaining a phenomenon (e.g., food consumption or nutrient intake). If parsimony is a goal in science, then why not stick to the single-measures approach? The answer is that researchers believe that all measures are fallible and that multiple measures of the same underlying concept will provide a more accurate representation of the underlying concept, if errors in measurement are independent (a basic assumption of classic test theory). Thus, a single composite index of knowledge (or beliefs) derived by some combination of individual items (e.g., simply summed) is likely to provide a more accurate and reliable estimate of the individual's nutrition knowledge than his or her response to any single item. So, instead of relating all measures of knowledge (i.e., each test item) to a dietary quality measure, for example, it is more parsimonious to take one summary measure of a concept and relate it to an outcome variable like nutrient intake.

Measuring Attitudes

Numerous techniques have been developed to measure attitudes. Three of the more common techniques--Thurstone, Likert, and semantic differential scales--are presented here in terms of the expectancy-value model. The underlying premise of each of these techniques is to assess an individual's overall evaluation of some object or act. Remember that attitude was defined as "a person's feelings toward and evaluation of some object, person, issue, or event" (Fishbein and Ajzen, 1975, pg 12), and that the distinguishing feature of an attitude was its affective or evaluative component. Each technique arrives at this assessment of an individual's overall evaluation by using different assumptions.

Thurstone Scaling. The first step in the development of a Thurstone scale of attitudes is to generate a set of belief statements associated with the attitude object. For example, suppose that the attitude object is eating at a fast-food restaurant. The researchers would conduct a pretest by asking a set of respondents (drawn from the same population as those respondents to be included in the main study) to list the advantages and disadvantages of eating at a fast-food restaurant. Suppose that the following set of beliefs was elicited: Eating at a fast-food restaurant means 1) getting food that is tasty, 2) getting food that is inexpensive, 3) getting food that is served quickly, 4) getting food that is not nutritious, 5) getting food that is greasy, and 6) getting food that is high in calories. Typically, a researcher developing a Thurstone scale would collect a large set of belief statements (often 30 or more) because a substantial number of these statements will be eliminated during the scale development.

The second step is to give all the belief statements to another group of respondents (also drawn from the same population as those respondents to be included in the main study) and have the individuals evaluate each belief statement by using a 9-point scale, ranging from extremely favorable to extremely unfavorable. In other words, individuals are asked to evaluate whether the belief statement reflects a favorable or unfavorable position on the topic. Those statements that are rated similarly across respondents (i.e., rated as the same or on adjacent scale points) are treated as "unambiguous" and selected for inclusion in the questionnaire. This selection procedure uses a "criterion of ambiguity" to determine which items to select for the questionnaire. Basically, this criterion identifies those items for which the majority of respondents evaluate in the same or adjacent categories. Edwards (1957) provides a very useful discussion of the specific algorithms for determining the ambiguity of an item. Each unambiguous item receives a scale value (based on the "average" category--from the 9-point scale--in which it was placed). The final questionnaire would be composed of a set of belief statements, ranging from a very favorable position on a topic to a very unfavorable position. In the final questionnaire, the respondent is asked whether he or she agrees or disagrees with each statement. Those scale values associated with the items with which the respondent agrees then are summed to provide a measure of the individual's attitude.

An example will help to illustrate the development of a Thurstone scale. Suppose that a researcher is interested in the respondent's attitude toward eating at a fast-food restaurant. By using the beliefs presented earlier, the investigators would present each belief statement to a group of respondents to evaluate (by using the 9-point, bipolar favorable/unfavorable scale scored for +4 to -4). Further suppose that each of the beliefs is unambiguous (i.e., the respondents rate each belief similarly) and that the following scale values are derived for each belief: getting food that is tasty (+4), getting food that is inexpensive (+2), getting food that is served quickly (+1), getting food that is high in calories (0), getting food that is greasy (-2), and getting food that is not nutritious (-3). Now that the specific beliefs and their associated scale values have been identified, the questionnaire to measure the respondents' attitudes toward eating at a fast-food restaurant can be developed. Respondents are given the list of belief statements and are asked whether they agree or disagree with each statement (i.e., a dichotomous judgment). Suppose that an individual agrees with the statements concerning taste (+4), inexpensive (+2), and not nutritious (-3). This person's overall attitude score would be +3 (4 + 2 - 3), which would be quite positive because the highest possible score using these beliefs and scale values would be +7. This score (+7) would be obtained if the respondent agreed with all the beliefs with a positive scale value and disagreed with all the beliefs with a negative scale value. The lowest attitude score for these beliefs with these scale values would be a -5.

Likert Scaling. The first step in the development of a Likert scale of attitude is the same as the first step described for the development of a Thurstone scale; that is, the identification of a set of beliefs associated with the attitude object. The second step in developing a Likert scale is for the researcher to determine whether the belief statement reflects a positive or negative value. Getting food that is tasty, a belief statement used previously, would reflect a positive value, whereas getting food that is greasy would reflect a negative value. Researchers eliminate those items that reflect a neutral value; that is, only those items that reflect either a positive or negative value are included in the questionnaire. The respondent is asked typically to rate each belief statement on a 5-point agree/disagree scale (which is usually scored from +2 to -2). The attitude measure is determined by summing the respondent's ratings across each belief question.

The researcher can determine what belief statements to include in the final instrument by applying the criterion of internal consistency (discussed in the previous section on measuring knowledge and beliefs). This criterion is used to examine the relationship of each belief statement with the total (summated) score. If each belief is an indicant of the underlying attitude, then the score on each belief should be highly correlated with the total (summated) score.

Conversely, if a particular belief is uncorrelated with the total score, then this belief is unlikely to be an indicant of the underlying attitude.

The assessment of the positive or negative value of the belief allows the researcher to determine *a priori* the direction in which the statement should be scored. For example, if an individual strongly disagrees with a belief that has a negative value, that response should contribute as much to the individual's overall attitude as a strong agreement with a belief statement that has a positive value. On a practical level, however, researchers rarely assess the value of a belief *a priori*. Rather, the researcher will examine the direction of the correlation of each individual item with the total score. If the correlation is negative, then the belief statement is scored incorrectly; that is, what the researcher initially perceived as a positive (or negative) value is perceived by the respondent as negative (or positive). The scoring on this item is simply reversed when calculating the total (attitude) score.

Semantic Differential Scaling. This attitude scaling technique has its roots in the work of Osgood, Suci, and Tannebaum (1957). A brief review of the development of the semantic differential will provide some foundation for the use of this technique to measure attitudes. Osgood and his colleagues examined the relationships among a large set of bipolar adjectives (e.g., good/bad, beneficial/harmful, pleasant/unpleasant, strong/weak, active/passive) by having individuals rate a wide set of concepts and objects (e.g., mother, boat, church) on each bipolar adjective. These researchers used factor analytic procedures to determine the underlying meaning of words and identified three fundamental dimensions--evaluation, potency, and activity. The relevant dimension for attitude measurement is evaluation.

One goal of the work by Osgood and colleagues (1957) was the development of a single, universal measure of attitudes that could be applied across cultures and across attitude objects. Unfortunately, no one semantic differential scale provides such a measure. This limitation is due to the potential confounding interaction between the meaning underlying the bipolar adjective and the concept being rated;

that is, the meaning of the bipolar adjective may change when used to rate different concepts. Empirically, this interaction can be detected by determining whether the bipolar adjectives have high loadings on the same (or different) dimensions when a factor analysis is conducted of the bipolar adjectives. For example, the bipolar adjectives of strong/weak seem to be representative of the evaluative dimension when used to rate the concept of horseradish (a food); that is, the strong/weak adjectives are likely to be highly correlated with adjective pairs that typically measure evaluation (e.g., good/bad, favorable/unfavorable adjectives). In contrast, the strong/weak bipolar adjectives seem to be representative of the potency dimension when used to rate the concept of smell. That is, the strong/weak adjectives are likely to be highly correlated with adjective pairs that typically measure potency (e.g., soft/hard, large/small adjectives).

Because of the potential confounding of a concept-by-scale interaction, researchers should determine the dimensions underlying the adjective pairs used to measure the attitude objects of interest. Typically, a factor analysis of the adjectives used to measure the attitude object would provide information concerning the underlying dimensions. At the very least, the researcher should select adjective pairs whose underlying meanings have been established from past factor analytic work. Simply inventing bipolar adjectives does not mean that the researcher is applying a semantic differential scale. The strength of the semantic differential scaling technique in measuring an attitude is in the ability of the researcher to determine the underlying (evaluative) meaning of the bipolar adjectives and not in the rating of the attitude object on any pair of adjectives. For example, rating a beer on bipolar adjectives such as filling/light and bubbly/flat does not imply that the researcher has measured the respondent's attitude because the underlying (evaluative) meaning of these adjective pairs is unknown.

<u>Comparison of the Three Methods.</u> The final outcome for each method is a measure of the respondent's evaluation of some object or act. The manner in which this measure is determined,

however, differs across the three methods. Both the Thurstone and semantic differential scales allow neutral belief statements, whereas the Likert scale eliminates neutral statements. Both the Thurstone and Likert scales require ratings (from either the respondents or the investigator) to select the belief statements to include in the questionnaire, whereas the semantic differential technique uses no formal selection procedure to identify these statements.

If the expectancy-value view is used to characterize these techniques, then both the Likert and semantic differential scales place relatively greater emphasis on the belief component of attitude than the Thurstone scale. That is, both the Likert and semantic differential scales allow for greater variation in beliefs than the Thurstone scale. Conversely, the Thurstone scale places greater emphasis on the evaluation of the belief than either the semantic differential or Likert scaling technique. For example, the Thurstone scaling described previously assesses evaluation by using a 9-point, favorable/unfavorable scale, whereas belief strength (expectancy) is measured by whether the respondent agrees or disagrees with the statement (i.e., a dichotomous judgment of belief strength). The Likert scale, on the other hand, assesses evaluation by having the researcher judge whether a statement is positive or negative (i.e., a dichotomous judgment of evaluation), whereas belief strength (expectancy) is measured on a 5-point, agree/disagree scale. Fishbein and Ajzen (1975) present a more detailed comparison of these scaling techniques.

Alternative Approaches Toward Measuring Attitude. In addition to these standard attitude scaling techniques, there are two alternative approaches for measuring attitude--the expectancy-value approach and the tripartite approach. Fishbein and Ajzen (1975, pg 6) use the expectancy-value model of attitudes in their Theory of Reasoned Action and define attitudes as "a learned predisposition to respond in a consistently favorable or unfavorable manner toward some object or act." Attitude is determined by the sum of the individual's salient beliefs (b_i) about the consequences of performing the behavior multiplied by the individual's evaluation (e_i) of the consequences. Fishbein and Ajzen express this relationship as follows:

$$\text{Attitude}_{(act)} = \Sigma b_i e_i. \qquad (3\text{-}1)$$

Belief strength (expectancy) is typically measured by using a 7-point, likely/unlikely scale. The evaluation (value) is typically measured by using a 7-point, good/bad scale. These measures often are assigned scores from +3 to -3. This procedure to assess attitudes makes several measurement assumptions. As several researchers have noted (e.g., Schmidt, 1973), the valid application of a multiplicative model assumes the use of ratio scales. That is, if the scales in a multiplicative model are interval level (i.e., scales which allow for a linear transformation such as adding a constant value), then any correlation of the model with other variables (e.g., behavior) is suspect. These authors demonstrate that linear transformations of interval-level data will result in widely different correlations between a multiplicative model and another variable. Thus, the use of nonratio scales in multiplicative models is problematic and may lead to unwarranted conclusions concerning the relationship between the multiplicative model and an external variable.

A second assumption in the use of the expectancy-value model is the bipolar scaling of both the belief and evaluation measures; that is, scoring each measure from +3 to -3. This bipolar scaling has several implications. First, if either the belief strength or the evaluation measure is neutral (i.e., 0), then that belief does not contribute toward the individual's attitude (i.e., the product of that belief times evaluation is 0). Second, this scoring implies that beliefs that are considered to be very unlikely (-3) and to be very bad (-3) make the same level of contribution toward an individual's attitude as do beliefs that are considered to be very likely (+3) and to be very good (+3) because the product for each belief results in a score of +9. Several researchers (e.g., Bettman, Capon, and Lutz, 1975; Lutz,

1975) provide evidence to support this bipolar scoring of both belief strength and the evaluation of the belief.

A third assumption underlying this integration rule is that the beliefs are independent of each other; that is, the summative rule does not allow for any interrelationship among the beliefs. The theoretical assumptions associated with this model are presented in the discussion of the Fishbein and Ajzen (1975) Theory of Reasoned Action in Chapter 6.

As we noted earlier, the tripartite approach conceptualizes attitudes as having three components--affect, cognition, and behavior. The tripartite view may be seen in an instrument used by Schutz, Moore, and Rucker (1977) to generate food-attitude factors for inclusion in their analysis of food purchase and use. This instrument includes 30 items about the "respondents' innovativeness and creativity in the preparation of foods, child-rearing practices, and feelings about food and eating" to which the respondent agreed or disagreed on a 7-point scale. Although they did not so indicate, their instrument reflects a tripartite definition of attitudes. When examining the 30 items, statements of affect as well as statements of beliefs and behavior are found. Although some of the statements were hard to classify, approximately two could be called statements of affect, 13 could be called statements of belief, and 15 could be called statements of behavior.

An example of an affect statement would be "I like to go grocery shopping." The verb "like" places this statement in the affective domain. On the other hand, the statement "creative cooking is an impossibility" is an example of the association between an object (creative cooking) and an attribute (an impossibility). Another example is "Most food packages are too large," where the object is most food packages and the attribute is too large. These last two statements and others included in their list can be classified as belief statements belonging to the cognitive domain. Lastly, "I serve hamburger or hot dogs once a week," where I is the object and serve hamburger or hot dogs once a week is the behavioral attribute can be defined as a belief statement, but it is a statement that belongs to the conative domain because it links a person to an action.

Relationship among Behavior, Knowledge, Beliefs, and Attitudes

Numerous investigations have been conducted to examine the relationship between food-related behavior and nutrition-related knowledge, beliefs, and attitudes. Researchers have attempted to measure many specific beliefs and attitudes (e.g., convenience, sensory-aesthetic, nutrition) and relate them to many types of behaviors (e.g., food consumption) or outcomes of behavior (e.g., dietary quality indexes) in many segments of the population (e.g., teenagers, vegetarians). Although a comprehensive review of this body of literature would be informative, it is beyond the scope of this chapter. Instead, a review of Bayton's (1966) conceptualization of how attitudes and beliefs are related to behavior is presented because it provides a cogent paradigm for approaching the study of the psychosocial determinants of food-related behavior. In addition, a discussion of meta-analysis is provided because it is a useful technique for integrating and evaluating empirical findings across studies.

Bayton's Paradigm. Bayton (1966) contends that consumers have a basic set of attitudes and beliefs which they use to determine their food choices and food rejections. Based on his experiences, he has observed that as a group, consumers use 22 specific attitudes and beliefs (which he calls parameters) to make food consumption decisions. Bayton (1966) believes that these 22 parameters can be grouped into seven categories: nutrition, economic, sensory-aesthetic, personableness, appropriateness, convenience, and health apprehensions. According to Bayton (1966), no one consumer will use all of these parameters, and in order to understand how people use these available parameters, three types of analysis are needed. Bayton's (1966) parameters and types of analysis are presented here at length for two reasons: 1) almost all of the attitudes and beliefs which have been studied by various investigators can be placed into one or more of these seven basic categories; thus, his categories provide a rather elegant conceptual outline, and 2) the types of analysis reflect three basic questions or hypotheses which researchers often pose concerning attitudes and beliefs.

Bayton's (1966) first category *nutrition* includes four parameters: 1) body growth needs, 2) general health needs, 3) vitality or energy needs, and 4) long-lasting energy needs. The second category *economic* contains two parameters--price *per se* and value (what you get for your money). *Sensory-aesthetic* has two parameters: a taste-aroma-appearance complex parameter and a refreshment parameter (which implies a coolness or relief of thirst). The fourth category *personableness* contains two parameters: 1) personableness-in-general, described as lively, good complexion, bright and sparkling eyes, general attractiveness, and 2) a sex personableness, which means for males masculinity, vigorous, and athletic, and for females femininity, lovely complexion, and nice figure. *Appropriateness* is the fifth category and is defined generally as appropriate for my kind of person or appropriate to a given situation. The three specific parameters in this appropriateness category include 1) age-group appropriateness (e.g., milk for children), 2) status-group appropriateness (e.g., wine is for yuppies), and 3) social-setting appropriateness (e.g., for special guests). The sixth category is *convenience*--specifically, convenience in purchasing (availability), convenience in storing, convenience in preparation, convenience in serving, and convenience in consumption. The seventh and final category is *health apprehensions*, and in this category Bayton (1966) includes four parameters 1) apprehensions about weight, 2) apprehensions about heart disease, 3) apprehensions about contamination of the food (e.g., pesticides), and 4) apprehensions about allergies.

To understand how people use these available parameters, Bayton (1966) says that three types of analysis must be used. He labels the different types of analysis "people profiles," "product profiles," and "discriminating influence." The people profiles is an analysis which attempts to discern which parameters are most important to a person when making decisions about food in general. The assumption is that not all 22 parameters will be equally important to all people. For instance, the three most important parameters for an individual might be 1) convenience in general, 2) economic, particularly price, and 3) taste-aroma-appearance. A person with this profile could be a graduate student with limited economic resources. Another individual could place great importance on 1) health apprehension, particularly weight, 2) personableness, especially the gender-related parameter, and 3) appropriateness, particularly social-setting appropriateness (i.e., with friends). A person with this profile could be a teenage girl.

The "product profiles" analysis is concerned with which of the parameters are associated with particular food products. For example, let's take fruits. The three top parameters associated with fruits could be 1) nutrition, especially the general health parameter, 2) sensory-aesthetic parameter, particularly refreshing, and 3) health apprehensions, perhaps related to weight (e.g., fruits are perceived as lower in kilocalories by many people).

The "discriminating influence" analysis seeks to discover which parameters are related to behavior. For example, a person may have many beliefs and attitudes related to a particular food product or food group, but only a few of them may actually influence his or her actions. The set of attitudes and beliefs (parameters) which influence behavior is called the "discriminating influence." Let's take a behavior like eating hamburgers at a fast-food restaurant as an example. After surveying 100 people, let's say we found that 70% of the respondents believed that eating at a fast-food restaurant was convenient and that 30% did not. Of the 70% who thought it was convenient, 50% had eaten hamburgers at this type of restaurant at least once in the past two weeks. Of the 30% who did not think eating at this type of restaurant was particularly convenient, 50% also had eaten there at least once in the same time period. This belief about convenience then would not be considered a discriminating influence on people's behavior because people with different beliefs behaved in a similar manner. However, if we found 50% of the people thought hamburgers from a fast-food restaurant were tasty, and of these, 90% had eaten at this type of restaurant in the past two weeks, compared to only 10% of the people who thought this type of food was not tasty, then the sensory-aesthetic parameter of tasty would be considered a discriminating influence. From this example, we can see that looking for the discriminating influence is looking for those attitudes and beliefs that influence behavior.

Meta-Analysis. Investigations undertaken to determine the relationship between dietary behavior and 1) nutrition knowledge and 2) food- and nutrition-related attitudes have provided ambiguous results. Some investigators have found a significant relationship between nutrition knowledge and dietary behavior (e.g., Hinton, Eppright, Chadderon, and Wolins, 1963; Seiler and Fox, 1973; Sims, 1978), whereas others have not (e.g., Byrd-Bredbenner and Shear, 1982; Grotkowski and Sims, 1978; Schwartz, 1975). Likewise, some investigators have found a significant relationship between food- and nutrition-related attitudes and dietary behavior (e.g., Sims, 1978; Byrd-Bredbenner and Shear, 1982; Schwartz, 1975), whereas others have not (e.g., Grotkowski and Sims, 1978).

One manner in which to resolve ambiguous findings in a subject area is to integrate the findings from published empirical studies. Typically, researchers integrate empirical findings through narrative reviews, that is, a visual inspection and integration of a set of research findings. The narrative review, however, has limitations. It lacks power to detect a relation where one exists (that is, it is susceptible to type 2 errors). In addition, the preconceived ideas that investigators may bring into a narrative review may bias their conclusions. A more systematic approach for integrating empirical findings is described as meta-analysis, which Glass, McGaw, and Smith (1981) define as the statistical analysis of a collection of findings from independent studies for the purpose of integrating those findings. Meta-analytic techniques (see Glass, McGaw, and Smith, 1981; Rosenthal, 1978, 1982) have been developed to allow researchers to address quantitatively two questions: Is there a relationship between two variables? And what is the strength (effect-size) of the relationship?

Axelson, Federline, and Brinberg (1985) is used to illustrate a meta-analysis and to summarize the relationship between dietary behavior and food- and nutrition-related knowledge and attitudes. In meta-analysis, the first step is to specify the theoretical relations to be examined. In this case, the relationship examined was between dietary behavior and food- and nutrition-related knowledge and attitudes.

The second step is to decide on the operational plan. A decision must be made about the sampling strategy (e.g., census or random) for collecting the empirical studies and about the information to be extracted and coded from each study for analysis. Axelson *et al.* (1985) only included in their meta-analysis those studies that met the following criteria: 1) Food- and nutrition-related attitudes or knowledge and dietary intake were measured for the same individual. 2) A correlation coefficient was calculated and reported between each of these variables. This criterion excluded studies, for example, that may have examined the relevant variables, but failed to report the actual statistical value obtained. Relevant information from the studies is coded just like in an empirical study.

The third step is to conduct the analysis of the coded empirical findings. Axelson *et al.* (1985) obtained a correlation coefficient between the two variables in question from each study. They then performed a test to determine whether there was a significant relation between the variables nutrition knowledge and dietary intake as well as between food- and nutrition-related attitudes and dietary intake. These relationships were significant ($p < 0.01$).

Because the relationships were significant, the effect-size (or degree of association) of the relations was estimated. The estimated effect-size of the knowledge and dietary intake relationship was $r = 0.10$, and the effect-size of the attitudes and dietary intake relationship was $r = 0.18$. We observed that, although the relations examined were significant, the estimates of the effect-sizes were small. These low estimates of effect-size probably are the result of poor measurement methods of the constructs rather than a lack of relationship between attitudes and behavior. For example, these estimates may reflect a lack of consideration for the dimensionality of the variables being measure, a lack of reliability or validity in the measurement of food- and nutrition-related knowledge and attitudes, and/or a lack of correspondence between the measures of dietary intake and knowledge or attitudes.

As discussed previously, investigators (Moxley and Wimberly, 1982; Sims, 1981) have reported that determining the dimensionality of the measurements of nutrition knowledge and attitudes is an important aspect of providing a more accurate description of these variables. Identification of the dimensions of each variable and keeping these dimensions separate in the analysis may improve the correspondence between the predictor and criterion variables. Lastly, investigators defined dietary intake, the criterion variable in these studies, as either dietary quality or nutrient intake. These measurements are really outcomes of a myriad of behaviors. Investigators who have more specifically defined the food-related behavior under study have found a greater effect-size between the predictor and criterion variables--e.g., the relationship between opinions about nutrition-related practices and practice scores ($r = 0.61$) (Jalso, Burns, and Rivers, 1965).

4

"There is evidence that food preference constitutes one of the strongest single predictors of food choices and food acceptance." (Meiselman, 1986, pg 236)

"The sensory-affective motivation for acceptance is basically equivalent to liking or disliking a food. Individual differences on sensory-affective grounds (e.g. liking or disliking lima beans) probably account for most variations in food preference within a culture." (Rozin and Vollmecke, 1986, pg 439)

These quotes by Meiselman (1986) and Rozin and Vollmecke (1986) are exceptions to the general state of affairs in the literature concerning food-related behavior. The inability of researchers to find strong associations between characteristics of individuals (e.g., nutrition knowledge, gender) and their food consumption usually prevents any definitive statements regarding the reasons for the observed variations in individuals' food-related behavior. Food preferences, however, seem to be the exception for two reasons. First, the hypothesized relationship between food preferences and food consumption has intuitive appeal--after all, it makes sense that people would tend to eat what they liked; that is, they would seek out the foods that give them pleasure. Second, many investigators have examined the relationship between preferences and consumption and found a positive one.

In this chapter, the concept of food preferences and its relation to food-related behavior will be examined. Because no set of
definitions related to food preferences is accepted generally by
researchers, the discussion of food preferences will start with an
examination of various definitions. This discussion is followed by an
examination of the relationship between preferences and consumption. Finally, the determinants of food preferences will be explored.

Definitions

The following definitions were chosen as the starting point for
discussion because they seem to represent the range of conceptualization of food preferences by investigators.

> "*Food consumption* is a behavioral act involving the
> acquisition of food. The word *acquisition* has been
> chosen deliberately to accommodate the common dis-
> crepancy in meaning of the word consumption as used
> by the economist and as used by the nutritionist. To
> the economist, food consumption denotes the
> *purchase*, or obtainment by other means, of food.
> Nutritionists, on the other hand, convey the meaning
> of *ingestion* in their use of food consumption. . .
> *Food acceptability* has an important distinction from
> food consumption despite the fact that they are often,
> erroneously, used interchangeably. Food acceptability
> denotes the consumption of food accompanied by
> pleasure ... *Food preference is ... the degree of like or
> dislike for a food ...* food preference is a phenomenon
> that rests predominantly in the realm of attitudes and
> can exist independently of consumption. An individ-
> ual is capable of having a definite preference for a
> food that he or she has never tasted." (Randall, 1982,
> pg 123-124)

> "A ... set of distinctions must be made among *use*, *pref-
> erence*, and *liking* ... The most common and 'objective'
> measure of food selection is *use*, i.e. what and how
> much a person eats ... *Preference* assumes the avail-
> ability of at least two different items, and refers to the
> choice of one rather than the other. *Liking* refers to a

set of hedonic (affective) reactions to a food, usually indexed directly by verbal reports or rating scales, but sometimes indirectly by facial expressions. Preference is ordinarily taken to be synonymous with liking, but this is not necessarily the case. Liking is only one of the motivations that may account for a preference. Perceived health value, convenience, and economic factors are potent influences on preferences ... but may not affect liking. A dieter, for example, may prefer cottage cheese to ice cream, but like ice cream better. Nonetheless, in most cases, we prefer those foods that we like better." (Rozin and Vollmecke, 1986, pg 434)

"A number of techniques are available to measure consumer likes and dislikes for food. Most of these techniques can be subsumed under the rubrics of 'preference,' 'acceptance' or 'consumption' measurement. Unfortunately, the definitions of these terms have varied considerably in the literature. For the purpose of this report, these terms are defined as (1) preference--the expressed degree of liking or disliking for a food when obtained in response to a food name; (2) acceptance--the expressed degree of liking or disliking for a food when obtained in response to a prepared sample of the food; and (3) consumption-- the number and/or amount of a food item(s) that is (are) actually ingested." (Cardello and Maller, 1982, pg 1553)

These lengthy quotes illustrate some of the issues that are involved when defining preferences. For example, is preference a choice or a stated liking or disliking for a product? Or, is preference a response to food that is eaten or a response to the name of a food? When examining the definitions, two key issues seem to emerge and explain most of the source of variation in these definitions. These issues are 1) the type of task or judgment that is required of the respondent (consumer) and 2) the type of stimulus the respondent must judge.

Table 4.1

Type of Stimulus versus Type of Task for
Measuring Affective Responses to Foods

| Task | Stimulus | |
	Food name	Food item
	Cell 1	**Cell 2**
Affective rating	Preference	Acceptability
scale--indicates	(Randall)	(Randall)
like/dislike	Preference	Acceptance
	(Cardello & Maller)	(Cardello & Maller)
	Liking	Liking
	(Rozin & Vollmecke)	(Rozin & Vollmecke)
	Cell 3	**Cell 4**
Choice rating scale--	Preference	Preference
indicates most liked	(Rozin & Vollmecke)	(Rozin & Vollmecke)
food given two or		
more choices		

In Table 4.1, the two most common types of tasks along with
the two most common types of stimuli are represented in a 2 x 2
matrix. The two most common tasks given to respondents are 1)
affective rating scales, anchored by terms indicating degree of liking
or disliking of a food stimulus (these scales are called hedonic scales),
and 2) choice rating scales, in which the respondent is asked to choose
one food he or she likes (prefers) the best from among two or more
food stimuli. The two most common stimuli used are 1) food names
and 2) actual food products (in some cases, pictures of foods are

used). In most cases, when actual food products are used as stimuli, the respondent is expected to taste each stimulus before responding.

In Table 4.1, four task-by-stimuli situations (cells) are presented: affect rating scale-by-food name, affect rating scale-by-food item, choice rating scale-by-food name, and choice rating scale-by-food item. Within each of these cells, the various investigators' definitions are placed according to how they seem to view the types of tasks and stimuli. For example, Randall (1982) defined preference as degree of like or dislike for a food and then indicated that a person may have a preference for a food that he or she may have never tasted. Hence, this definition indicates that an actual food item may not have to be present for a preference to be measured and that preference can be measured for a single item (cell 1) (i.e., a choice is not necessarily involved). On the other hand, Randall (1982) defines acceptability in such a way to indicate that it is a measure of liking for a particular food item when it is eaten. Cardello and Maller's (1982) definitions explicitly state that the difference between preference and acceptance is in the type of stimulus used when measuring degree of liking. In contrast to Randall (1982) and Cardello and Maller (1982), Rozin and Vollmecke (1986) make the distinction between preference and liking based on the type of task required of the respondent. Preference, according to Rozin and Vollmecke (1986), indicates choice and may or may not reflect degree of liking, whereas liking is an affective (hedonic) reaction to food. They do not specify types of stimuli in their definition.

To perhaps clarify the relationship among the preceding terms and their definitions, an examination of the manner in which food sensory specialists study people's reactions to food may be helpful. The test methods used by sensory experts are commonly grouped into three broad categories, depending on the information that is sought from respondents about a food product(s): 1) discriminative tests, which are used to determine whether there is a perceived difference among products, 2) descriptive tests, which are used to determine primarily the perceived characteristics of the products, and 3) affective tests, which are used to determine whether consumers like the products (Stone and Sidel, 1985). According to Stone and Sidel (1985, pg 227), affective testing means

> "measuring liking or preference for a product. Preference is that expression of appeal of one product versus another. Preference can be measured directly by comparison of two or more products with each other, that is, which of two or more products is preferred. Indirect measurement of preference is achieved by determining which product is significantly more liked than another product in a multiproduct test. There is an obvious and direct relationship between measuring product liking/acceptance and preference. To be more efficient, sensory evaluation should emphasize measuring product liking/acceptance in multiproduct tests and from these data determine preference. Scaling methods allow us to directly measure degree of liking and to compute preference from these data."

According to Stone and Sidel (1985) then, preference implies choice, but it can be measured directly or indirectly. It can be determined directly by having respondents compare products or indirectly by having respondents rate their degree of liking for various products. Based on the indirect method, the investigator needs to make inferences about comparative liking for products by examining the responses on the rating scales.

Various terms--preference, liking, acceptance--are used at times interchangeably and at other times to refer to different task/stimulus situations. Sensory scientists most often use the more inclusive term, affective, to refer to all of these task/stimulus situations. Although a consensus has not developed on which term is most appropriate for each situation, the distinctions made by these investigators are important. If data were collected from the same set of respondents for the same set of foods by using the four task/stimulus situations, the four sets of measures would not necessarily converge;

that is, these four types of measures may represent different constructs. From Stone and Sidel's (1985) comments, we would expect correspondence between measures from cells 1 and 3 and between measures from cells 2 and 4. Whether a person is asked to rate two products individually on a like/dislike scale, or whether a person is asked to indicate the more preferred of the two products, the results should be similar--the best liked product should have a higher rating on the scale or should be the one indicated as the best liked. These authors do not provide any information to determine whether differences would occur for the types of stimuli judged (i.e., cells 1 & 2 versus cells 3 & 4).

Cardello and Maller (1982) examined the relationship between measures obtained by having respondents rate nine food names on a 9-point, like/dislike scale (cell 1) and then 6-8 weeks later having them rate the nine foods on the same type of scale after tasting a food sample (cell 2). Based on the responses of 359 adults to the nine foods in the two situations, they found a positive but weak relationship (correlation coefficient of 0.30) between the two measures across all foods. When they examined the relationship between measures for each food item, however, only one significant relationship (for liver and onions) was found.

This lack of convergence between measures representing cell 1 and cell 2 is not particularly surprising because the food product that a person imagines when responding to a food name may not correspond to an actual food product presented to him or her for evaluation. This situation is probably very familiar to all of us--most of us have ordered a food item in a restaurant and were disappointed when we tasted the actual product. Our actual experience did not correspond to our expectations. We would hypothesize that the relationship between measures representing cells 3 and 4 would follow a similar pattern as those from cells 1 and 2.

Cardello and Maller (1982) also found that the three most preferred foods (whole milk, bacon, hash browns), determined by mean ratings on the hedonic scale, had lower mean ratings when the actual foods were presented; in addition, the three least preferred foods (liver and onions, lima beans, skimmed milk) were rated higher when the actual foods were presented. Lastly, the three foods (tomato juice, frankfurters, pork and beans) in the middle had mean ratings that were very similar for both preferences and acceptability. Cardello and Maller (1982, pg 1556) interpreted these findings as

> "It is, as if, our stated preferences for foods reflect a quintessential or idealized image or memory trace of the food, and that actual preparations of the food item are never as good or as bad as this mental image ... The relationship between preference and acceptance ratings for 'liked' and 'disliked' items conflicts with .. [others'] ... interpretation that hedonic preference ratings reflect the respondent's opinion of the best preparation of the food item. While the present data support such an interpretation for preferred food items, it is clear from these data that preference ratings of nonpreferred items reflect the respondent's opinion of the 'worst' preparation of the food."

An alternate interpretation of Cardello and Maller's (1982) findings that the most preferred foods get lower acceptance ratings when they are actually tasted and the least preferred foods get higher acceptance ratings when they are actually tasted probably reflects a statistical property called *regression towards the mean*. Regression towards the mean is found whenever items are subdivided according to their ratings into high, medium, and low categories. When the items are rated again on the same or similar construct, their scores tend to regress towards the mean. This phenomenon is found for both biological and psychological measures. Therefore, this regression towards the mean of the preference data implies that psychological processes of the respondents are not needed to explain changes in their food preferences.

Probably the ideal situation would be to create terms which correspond specifically to each one of the four task/stimuli situations and one term to refer to the more inclusive concept. From the preceding discussion, there seems to be a greater difference between situations in columns one (cells 1 and 3) and two (cells 2 and 4) than between situations in rows one (cells 1 and 2) and two (cells 3 and 4). Therefore, for the remainder of this section, *food preferences* will be used to refer to task/stimuli situations in cells 1 and 3; that is, to the response by consumers to food names regardless of task type (i.e., like/dislike scale or a forced choice). *Food acceptance* will be used to refer to task/stimuli situations in cells 2 and 4; that is, to the response by consumers to actual food items regardless of task type. The term *sensory-related affect* will be used to refer to the more inclusive concept that encompasses the task/stimuli situations outlined in Table 4.1. The term *affective tests* will be used to refer to the techniques used to measure the concept of sensory-related affect.

Exactly what is sensory-related affect? When investigators ask about a person's preference or acceptance concerning a food, are they asking people to give their overall evaluation of that food or are they asking for some more specific evaluation? In other words, are preferences and acceptances just terms used for attitudes when food is the object or are they terms which refer to a sensory-related component which contributes to a person's attitude or overall evaluation of the object?

The definitions given by Randall (1982), Rozin and Vollmecke (1986), and Cardello and Maller (1982) seem to place food preferences and acceptances, either explicitly or implicitly, within the affective domain in that they use descriptions such as like or dislike of a food, eating with pleasure, or a set of hedonic (affective) reactions to a food. These authors, however, do not address the issue of how food preferences and acceptances are related to attitudes. Recall from the previous chapter that attitudes were defined as "a person's feeling toward and evaluation of some object, person, issue, or event" (Fishbein and Ajzen, 1975, pg 12). Shepherd (1987, pg 387) states that "sensory attributes of foods may be thought to influence a person's choice of whether to buy or eat that food. However, the composition and sensory attributes of the food will operate only through the person's preference for (attitude towards) that sensory attribute. Hence two people may perceive samples as equally high in saltiness intensity, but one person may like that level of saltiness in that food whereas the other may not. It is only by understanding the preferences (or attitudes) of the individuals that the role of sensory factors of food choice may be understood."

Shepherd's (1987) comments, although not stated explicitly, indicate that preferences and acceptances are used to refer to the overall sensory evaluation of the food, where *sensory evaluation* means the set of responses by an individual to the appearance, texture, and flavor of the food. Even when investigators ask individuals whether they like or dislike a food, they seem to be referring to or wanting to ask the individuals for their overall attitude towards a food based on their sensory evaluation. Do individuals, however, respond to the question using sensory characteristics?

Fewster, Bostian, and Powers (1973) conducted a study to determine whether common underlying dimensions or meanings of foods could be identified. They asked approximately 100 adults to rate seven foods or food groups on 38 semantic differential scales. Using factor analytic techniques, they examined the individuals' responses to the scales across all foods. These investigators extracted four factors and labeled them evaluative, communications, nutrition, and health apprehensions. The evaluative factor is the one of interest here. The terms and phrases which were related most significantly to this factor were appetizing (factor loading of 0.85), tasty (0.84), appealing (0.84), I like this food (0.82), satisfying (0.79), interesting (0.76), superior (0.72), liked by almost everybody (0.69), most of my friends like this food (0.67), I frequently use this food (0.64), and pleasant odor (0.61). Looking at the terms--appetizing, tasty, appealing, I like this food--which loaded the highest on this factor, one can see that Fewster *et al.*'s (1973) evaluative factor seems to capture a sensory dimension of meaning.

Measures of preference and acceptance seem to tap an individual's overall sensory evaluation of a food. Consequently, if food preference and acceptance can be considered a particular type of attitude (i.e., sensory-related affect) and if this type of attitude is an important component of a person's overall attitude toward a food, then we would expect sensory-related affect and attitudes to be related. Tuorila (1987a) examined the relationship between food acceptance (hedonic responses to food stimuli) and attitudes in three separate studies. In one study, respondents were asked to rate the pleasantness of sweetness in soft drinks that varied in color, flavor, and sucrose content (5% and 9%). In addition, respondents rated 1) the importance of healthiness in soft drinks, 2) the importance of reduced sugar content in soft drinks, and 3) their attitude (favorable/unfavorable) towards sugar. Tuorila did not find any relationship between the respondents' hedonic ratings of soft drinks containing 9% sucrose and their reported perceptions of healthiness and sugar content as related to soft drinks or their attitude towards sugar. The respondents' attitudes (healthiness, sugar content, and sugar), however, were significantly correlated (correlation coefficients ranged from 0.19 to 0.43) to their hedonic responses to soft drinks containing 5% sucrose. Even though Tuorila gives an explanation for these data, the finding of no relationship to a significant but weak relationship between hedonic responses and attitudes should not be surprising. In this situation, the lack of correspondence in measurements would predict no to only a weak relationship; that is, respondents' ratings of the pleasantness of sweetness in soft drinks would not necessarily correspond to their attitude towards sugar.

In two other studies by Tuorila (1987a), Fishbein and Ajzen's Theory of Reasoned Action (1975) was employed. Various components of this model were measured and related to food preference and acceptance measures. One aspect of Fishbein and Ajzen's model (which will be discussed in detail in Chapter 6) is that an emphasis is placed on corresponding psychosocial measures to behavioral measures. For example, if a measure of the pleasantness of sweetness in soft drinks is used, then the corresponding measure would be an attitude towards soft drinks and not sugar. This research design would provide a stronger test for the relationship between various measures of interest.

In one study, Tuorila measured consumers' hedonic responses to breads with normal and low levels of salt and related these hedonic responses to their 1) attitudes towards low-salt bread (the sum of 10 beliefs and their evaluations; i.e., $\Sigma b_i e_i$), 2) subjective norm (role of nutrition-related recommendations), 3) intentions to buy low-salt bread, and 4) actual selection of breads during the experimental period. Significant relationships among individuals' hedonic responses and their attitudes (correlation coefficient of 0.36), subjective norm (0.46), buying intentions (0.61), and selection (0.50) were found.

Finally, Tuorila (1987a) studied the relationship of consumers' acceptance (degree of liking actual products) and preferences ("survey" reports of liking) of milks with varying fat contents to their attitudes, buying intentions, and actual use of the various types of milk. Both the consumers' acceptance and preference ratings of the milks were significantly related (with one exception) to their attitude towards the milk. Interestingly, however, the correlation coefficients between the preference ratings and their attitudes toward nonfat (0.79), low-fat (0.64), and regular-fat milk (0.81) were higher than the acceptance ratings and their attitudes toward nonfat (0.60), low-fat (0.20, n.s.), and regular-fat milk (0.43). The relationship of the consumers' acceptance and preference ratings and their buying intentions and actual use of the various milks showed a similar pattern of correlations, although the correlation coefficients tended to be lower. The results of this last study correspond to the expected pattern of relationships among the various variables examined. From the previous discussion in this chapter on food preference and acceptance, the strongest relationship should be between preferences and attitude and the next strongest between acceptance and attitude. In addition, individuals' preferences and acceptances should be more strongly related to their attitudes than to their intention to act in a certain manner or to their actual behavior.

In summary, affective tests seem to measure an individual's overall sensory evaluation of a food. This overall sensory evaluation can be seen as one component of an individual's attitude toward a food. As Rozin and Vollmecke (1986) said, an individual's perception of the health, convenience, and economic values of the food also may have an important influence on what he or she chooses to eat. Consequently, a sensory-related affect measure may not correspond perfectly with a person's choice of a food, and the strength of this relationship will probably vary with the individual and the particular food under study.

Relationship Between Sensory-Related Affect and Consumption

According to the definition of *sensory-related affect* developed previously, food preferences and acceptances are an individual's over-all sensory evaluation of a food product, which can either be elicited in response to a food name or in response to an actual food item. The systematic study of the relationship of food preferences and acceptances to food consumption began in the 1940s and '50s through the U.S. Army Quartermaster Food and Container Institute (Stone and Sidel, 1985). Names like J. Kamenetzky, D.R. Peryam, F.J. Pilgrim, and H.G. Schutz are most commonly associated with this work. More recently (during the 1970s and 1980s), a significant number of studies concerning the relationship of taste (i.e., salty, sour, sweet, and bitter) attributes to food consumption have appeared in the scientific literature. According to Mattes and Mela (1986), the three most common characteristics of taste under investigation are taste thresholds, perceived intensity ratings, and preferences (i.e., affective tests). Investigators of taste characteristics hypothesize that taste may help regulate or play a role in maintaining an adequate intake of some dietary components. Up to this point, taste thresholds and perceived intensity ratings have not shown much promise as predictors of dietary intakes; however, taste preference and acceptance may have some predictive value for some dietary components, e.g., taste preference for sweetness and carbohydrate intake (Mattes and Mela, 1986). Even though the work related to taste preferences is quite interesting, it is a subject in itself and no attempt will be made to review it here.

When Cardello and Maller (1982) reviewed studies that examined the relationship between preferences and consumption, they found a wide range of correlation coefficients reported (from 0.20s to 0.80s), indicating that food preferences seem to account for a significant amount of variance in food consumption. These authors, however, did not attempt to draw conclusions about the relationship between acceptance and consumption because of the lack of research done in the area. Of the few studies that they did review, all indicated a positive relationship between acceptance measurements and consumption, but whether acceptance is a better predictor of consumption than preferences is not clear.

At this point, the reasons behind the wide range in the strength of the relationship between sensory-related affect measures and consumption found among studies have not received systematic analysis. Cardello and Maller (1982) in their brief review cite some possible reasons; for example, the differences in populations studied (e.g., military versus civilian), differences between measurements obtained in the laboratory and in the field, differences among task/stimuli situations, differences in measurement of consumption (e.g., proportion of food servings eaten versus proportion of individuals choosing the food item), and differences among food items--i.e., the relationship may be stronger for some types of foods like desserts than for others like breads.

Underlying many of these issues is the concept of *correspondence* in measurements between the predictor and criterion variables. Although a more detailed discussion of correspondence issues is presented in Chapter 6, a brief examination of these issues will provide insights into the measurement of sensory-related affect.

Ajzen and Fishbein (1980) note that an investigator needs to consider four basic factors--target, action, context, and time--when examining the relationship between psychosocial (predictor) variables and behavioral (criterion) variables. By target, Ajzen and Fishbein (1980) mean that the investigators must consider whether they are interested in a single instance of a category (e.g., apple) or a general category (e.g., fruit). Similarly, by action, Ajzen and Fishbein (1980) mean that the investigator must consider whether they are interested in a single action (e.g., eating apples) or a general behavioral category (e.g., eating fruit). Obviously, a stronger relationship will be found when the predictor variable (preference for eating apples) corresponds to the criterion variable (eating apples) in the level of specificity of the target and action.

Although Meiselman (1986) does not use the same terminology as Ajzen and Fishbein (1980), he is referring to this lack of correspondence in measurement of action when discussing possible sources of variation in the sensory-related affect and consumption relationship. He explains that differences will arise when hedonic scales rather than preferred frequency scales are used. A preferred frequency scale generally asks the respondents how often they would like to eat a food (i.e., sensory-related affect measured by asking about how they think they will act) rather than how much they like a food (i.e., sensory-related affect measured by asking how they feel about a food). A preferred frequency measure should correspond better with a frequency measure of consumption. Meiselman (1986) goes on to discuss the relationship between these two types of scales. He (1986, pg 236) says that

> "The two scales, hedonic and preferred frequency, differ in fundamental concept and correlate only moderately for most foods. Individual foods can be of relatively high hedonic preference but of relatively low preferred frequency (e.g. desserts), or of moderate hedonic preference but of higher preferred frequency (e.g. beverages)."

Embedded in the measurement of preference, acceptance, and consumption is the concept of <u>time</u>. An individual's stated preference will more likely correspond to his or her actions when the measures are taken close in time.

Lastly, <u>context</u> must be considered. Context is the environment in which the action takes place. When Cardello and Maller (1982) mentioned the laboratory versus the field setting as a possible confounding variable in interpreting the strength of the sensory-related affect/consumption relationship, they were referring to context effects. For example, Birch (1979) assessed the preference and consumption of snacks by preschool children at a nursery school and found a very strong relationship ($r = 0.80$) between the two variables. In this study, preference and consumption measurements were taken on the same day, and the children were limited in their choice of snack foods to those under study. Thus, a very strong relationship between preference and consumption was found in a laboratory-type setting (context), with measures taken on the same day (time), when the preference and consumption measures corresponded (action and target).

On the other hand, Randall and Sanjur (1981), in a mailed questionnaire, asked approximately 100 women to indicate their preferences for 20 vegetables. Preference was measured on a 5-point, hedonic scale, and frequency of consumption was measured on a 5-point scale, which ranged for zero (never consumed) to five (eaten almost daily). In this case, the target was the same for both the preference and consumption measures; however, the context, action, and time for the respondents were not specified. The correlation coefficients (Kendall's tau rank-order) between preference and consumption for each vegetable ranged from 0.30 to 0.62, indicating significant relationships; however, carrots and potatoes were the exception with correlation coefficients of 0.09 and 0.13, respectively. These correlation coefficients were lower than Birch's (1979), which would be expected because the context, time, and action were not specified clearly.

Randall and Sanjur (1981) noticed that, when the vegetables were arranged according to preference, the strength of the relationship between preference and consumption was inversely related to the preference ratings for the vegetable. In other words, the 11 most preferred vegetables had the lowest correlation coefficients (0.09 to 0.39) and the nine least preferred vegetables had the highest correlation coefficients (0.40 to 0.62). Randall and Sanjur (1982, pg 156) interpreted these findings to mean

> "that preferences serve to limit the available food supply for individuals, with dislike being associated with a food's noninclusion. Food selections would then be made from among the numerous foods that are well liked. Factors other than the strength of the preference for these foods would then determine ultimate food selections."

These investigators come rather close to arguing that food preferences are a necessary but not sufficient condition for food consumption, meaning that an individual must like a food before it will be consumed, but liking a food does not guarantee consumption.

Determinants of Sensory-Related Affect

Investigators studying the acquisition of food preferences and acceptances are at the vortex of the nature versus nurture argument; that is, is sensory-related affect an innate trait or is it one that is acquired through experience and socialization? The genetic- biological versus social-environmental questions can be asked at two levels of human development. One level concerns the *historical development of societies*. Some representative questions at this level are: 1) How did societies discover which animal and plant products in their environment were edible? 2) How did they come to eat, without the knowledge of nutrition science, an appropriate mix of products which allowed them to sustain life and reproduce? 3) How did they come to reject as inedible some animal and plant products that we know are edible? The other level concerns the *observed differences among societies and among individuals within a society.* Some representative questions at this level are: 1) Why do societies vary in their food preferences and acceptances? 2) Do individuals' preferences and acceptances change during their life time? 3) Why do individuals living in the same culture and even in the same family display different food preferences and acceptances? This section on determinants of sensory-related affect emphasizes the issues related to the last question--why do individuals within a culture and even within a family display different preferences and acceptances. The reader is directed to The *Psychobiology of Human Food Selection* (Barker, 1982) for some discussions on the issues raised by the other questions.

Before proceeding to the question of whether food preferences and acceptances are the result of innate biological traits or of learned social behavior, two general questions about people's chemical senses, taste and smell, should be answered. First, can children detect odor and taste stimuli? Infants, from birth, are responsive to taste (Cowart, 1981) and odor stimuli (Engen, 1986). In fact, Engen (1986) thinks that infants and adults can perceive differing odor intensities equally well. Second, do children and adults have the same likes and dislikes for odorants and tastants? Infants appear to have an innate preference for sweet tastes and to have an innate aversion for sour and bitter tastes. Salty taste appears, however, to elicit a hedonically neutral response from infants (Cowart, 1981). In comparison, most adults have a hedonically positive response to sweet and mild salty tastes, but most do not find bitter, sour, and strong salty tastes pleasant (Cowart, 1981). In contrast to tastants, Engen (1986) believes that infants do not have any innate preferences for odors at birth. The experimental evidence indicates that preferences for odors may start to develop in children when they are about 12 months old, and as they grow older, their odor preferences become more and more like adults' odor preferences. Both Cowart (1981) and Engen (1986) note that individuals vary significantly in their taste and odor preferences. Cowart (1981) believes that development of taste preferences may be a function of both biological and social factors, and the way in which these factors exert their influence awaits elucidation. On the other hand, Engen (1986) believes that the ability to perceive odor is present at birth, but odor preferences are learned.

If social-environmental and/or genetic-biological factors are involved in the development of sensory-related affect, a family resemblance in food preferences should be expected. The upper limit for the social and/or biological contributions to food preferences and acceptances should be the degree of similarity found among family members (e.g., the degree of similarity in food preferences of parent and child). Birch (1980b) assessed the relationship between 128 preschool children's food acceptances and those of their parents by having each child and his or her parents evaluate independently the same set of foods. She (1980b) then calculated a rank-order correlation coefficient (tau) for each child-mother and child-father pair. In addition, she examined the relationship between the acceptances of each child and a pseudo parent (unrelated adult in the sample). The median tau coefficients for the child-mother, child-father, and child-pseudo parent pairs were 0.14., 0.07, and 0.07, respectively. These results indicate that there is no significant relationship between the food acceptances of children and their parents. Birch (1980b) observed, however, that the pattern of distribution of tau coefficients (i.e., most were low, < 0.30, but positive) indicated a weak but positive relationship between the food acceptances of children and their parents. In comparison, the child-parent tau-coefficients were not significantly different from those of the child-unrelated adult tau values, which Birch interpreted as meaning that "the low correlation noted between parents' and children's preferences in the present study may be simply a reflection of a commonalty of preference within a subcultural group."

Pliner and Pelchat (1986) observed that 1) children usually have long-term, intimate contact with family members and 2) children share with each of their parents as well as their siblings some common genetic components. Either of these social and biological factors could be expected to exert a powerful influence on children's food preferences; that is, either of these factors could produce a resemblance among children's food preferences and those of their parents and siblings. Furthermore, Pliner and Pelchat (1986) think that, when both the social and biological factors are considered, young children should be expected to resemble their siblings more than their parents in their food preferences because the children are more similar in age and in genetic composition to their siblings than to their parents.

Pliner and Pelchat (1986) designed a study to investigate resemblance in food preferences between a group of young children and 1) their parents and 2) their siblings. Participating in the study were 55 families, composed of two parents and at least two children (the "target" children ranged in age from 24 to 83 months). Preferences for 139 food items were completed by the mother for all family members. A reliability check on the mothers' responses indicated a 74% agreement between child and mother (i.e., nearly three-quarters of the mothers' reports of their children's food preferences coincided exactly with the children's reports) and an 86% agreement between father and mother.

The children's food preferences were more similar to members of their own family (mean ϕ-coefficient $= 0.30$) than to members of a pseudo family ($\phi = 0.13$). A pseudo family was created for a child by randomly pairing him or her with an unrelated family. Moreover, children more closely resembled their siblings ($\phi = 0.50$) than either their mothers (0.20) or fathers (0.20). The relationships between the children and their pseudo siblings, mothers, and fathers were 0.17, 0.09, and 0.11, respectively. (Note: All of the coefficients were statistically significant at $p < 0.01$.) These findings corresponded to their predictions that young children should resemble their siblings more than their parents. Pliner and Pelchat (1986), however, did point out that children resembled unrelated children and adults, even though the resemblance was not as great as the family resemblance.

To examine the resemblance between adult children and their parents' food preferences, Pliner (1983) had 105 college students and their parents rate 47 foods on a 7-point like/dislike scale. The 47 foods represented commonly eaten meats, fish, poultry, eggs, dairy products, vegetables, and cereal and grain products. To ascertain the degree of agreement between children and their parents, she calculated Pearson product-moment correlation coefficients (r). Mean correlation coefficients for each child-mother, child-father, child-pseudo mother, and child-pseudo father pair were 0.25, 0.25, 0.12, and 0.11, respectively. All were statistically significant. Pliner (1983) concluded that even though the food preferences of the students resembled their parents as well as unrelated adults, there was a greater degree of agreement between the students and their parents. She also observed a trend in that the male and female students were more likely to resemble the same-sex parent than the opposite-sex parent. That is, the female child-mother coefficient was 0.29, male child-father was 0.30, female child-father was 0.20, and male child-mother was 0.22.

These studies of family resemblance indicate a weak to moderate relationship between parents and children in food preferences. As mentioned before, the results of these studies can give us an indication of the upper limit on the role that social or biological factors play, but they cannot tell us what role each of the factors is playing. There are a few research reports that have addressed the role of genetics in sensory-related affect. A recent study by Rozin and Millman (1987) provides an illustration of research in this subject area. They examined the food preferences as well as some other attitudes of 72 sets of twins, of which 38 were monozygotic (MZ) twins and 34 were same-sex dizygotic (DZ) twins. If genetics plays a role in the development of food preferences, then the expectation is that monozygotic twins will have a significantly greater resemblance than dizygotic twins. Rozin and Millman (1987) found that the twins did resemble each other more (mean r = 0.46 for MZ and 0.37 for DZ) than randomly paired (unrelated) twins (mean r = 0.20). Even though the pattern of the mean correlation coefficients of the monozygotic and dizygotic twins was in the expected direction, it was not statistically significant. These investigators concluded that their results conform to the findings of the majority of other investigators; namely, there seems to be a minimal genetic component in the development of food preferences or attitudes.

If sensory-related affect is not strongly determined by genetic-biological factors, then it must be determined by social-environmental factors. The research examining the social-environmental influences on sensory-related affect can be divided into two types based on research design. In the first type, researchers employ experimental designs (in which the independent variables are manipulated) aimed at determining how food preferences and acceptances are acquired. In the second type, researchers employ observational designs (in which the independent variables are observed) that describe the sensory attributes associated with sensory-related affect.

Experimental Approach. Very little research using the experimental approach has been conducted. The research in this area has been guided by two paradigms or views--one view is commonly called the "mere exposure effect" and the other can be called a social learning view.

The mere exposure effect is "the enhancement of positive affect toward a given object, [which] arises merely as a result of repeated stimulus exposure" (Zajonc and Markus, 1982, pg 125). In other words, the more often individuals are exposed to an object, the more positive their feelings are toward the object. The phenomenon of mere exposure has been demonstrated for many different types of objects in many different contexts (Zajonc, 1968). Investigators, however, do not agree on the reason or underlying mechanism for this observed effect. At the heart of the discussion is whether individuals can develop positive feelings toward an object without cognitive processes or whether individuals undergo some cognitive processing of an object before they can develop feelings for it. Many researchers have assumed that beliefs or knowledge about an object must come before a preference can develop. Zajonc and Markus (1982) believe, however, that preferences are, for the most part affectively-based phenomena and that, in some cases, affect or preference for an object may come before cognitive evaluation of the object. That is, people's beliefs about an object may occur after the preferences have been developed. Their argument is that in some circumstances an individual will develop a liking for an object and then will come to know it. For example, when a person is asked why she likes something, she will respond by saying it has this set of attributes or that set of attributes, but in reality the individual learned about the attributes after coming to like the object (e.g., a food) and is using them as justification for her liking.

The issue as it relates to sensory-related affect is whether individuals can develop a liking for a food with repeated experience (exposure) and then learn about it, or do individuals have to learn about a food before they come to like it. At this time, few studies have examined the effect of repeated exposure to a food on sensory-related affect. Pliner's (1982) study serves as an example here. The purpose of her experiment was to determine whether a mere exposure effect could be demonstrated when using a food stimulus. Using a within-subject design, she gave college students varying amounts of exposure to different food juices. On the pretext of an experiment designed to measure individual differences in ability to detect bitter taste, 24 students tasted 35 samples (randomly presented) of tropical fruit juice and rated them for bitterness (exposure phase of the study). Subjects were led to believe that each of the 35 samples was different (food coloring was added randomly to help disguise similar juices), when actually there were only three fruit juices presented to each subject: one was presented 20 times, one 10 times, and one 5 times (Note: each subject did not receive one of the four juices which in effect made one juice presented zero times). Presentation of the juices was counterbalanced so that each juice was presented to an equal number of subjects. The four types of juices were selected based on pretest results that they were not very familiar and that they were very similar to one another in terms of liking and bitterness. Affective responses were measured twice. Subjects were asked to taste and rate their liking on a 7-point hedonic scale for the three juices tasted in the exposure phase and one juice that they had never tasted. Subjects returned one week later and rated the same juices again.

Pliner (1982) found that the more frequently the students were exposed to a juice, the more they reported liking the juice. Thus, she demonstrated the mere exposure effect with a food as an object. This positive affective response was short-lived, however; by the second session, the students did not report a significantly better liking for the juice to which they had the greatest exposure. Considering the brief experimental treatment, this short-term effect is understandable.

Examples of research studies in which a social learning paradigm was employed to examine the development of food preferences and acceptances are found in work conducted by Birch and her colleagues (Birch, 1980a; Birch, Birch, Marlin, and Kramer, 1982). In one study, Birch (1980a) investigated the effect of peers on the liking of vegetables of preschool children. First, the 39 children's preferences for nine vegetables were assessed. Based on this assessment, the target children were seated at lunch for four days with children that differed from the target children's preferences for the vegetables. After the experimental period, the target children's preferences for previously less preferred vegetables increased, demonstrating an effect of peer modeling.

In another study, Birch and her colleagues (1982) examined the use of food as an instrumental component of a contingency, hypothesizing that the preference for a food which is used as an instrumental component of a contingency would decrease. An example of using food in this way is when a parent says to a child, you can't have dessert until you eat your squash, where eating the squash is the instrumental activity and eating dessert is the contingent activity. In this experiment with 12 preschool children, fruit juice was the instrumental activity and play was the contingent activity. As predicted, these researchers found that the children's preferences for the fruit juice decreased when used as an instrumental component of a contingency.

Birch and her colleagues have been studying the development of sensory-related affect and eating behavior in preschool children for about ten years. The reader is referred to a recently published review of the work (Birch, 1987).

Observational Approach. For the most part, food sensory specialists and social psychologists have examined preferences in a similar manner: both have used the expectancy-value view of beliefs and attitudes. They have tried to understand why individuals prefer some foods to others by examining the attributes of each of the foods (e.g., food A has more fat than food B) and then determining how important each attribute is in explaining the overall evaluation (i.e., liking) of each food. Researchers using this approach make two key assumptions (Zajonc and Markus, 1982). First, they assume that the observed preference for one object (food) over another object can be explained by the weighted importance (evaluation) of the attributes of each object. Second, they assume that these attributes are the same ones that allow individuals to detect, discriminate, recognize, and categorize the objects. Researchers using this approach base their analysis of preferences on the analysis of the attributes associated with the objects. In other words, they study the cognitive representations (i.e., beliefs) of the objects' attributes, which they think have some affect (evaluation) linked to them. Zajonc and Markus (1982) question the assumption on which this approach is based, namely that the affect contained in preferences comes necessarily after cognitive processing. They say that this assumption implies that a preference is acquired after the cognitive coding of the specific attributes of the object, after the evaluation of the attributes, and after the integration of the individual's cognitive and affective responses to the object, which ultimately represents the person's overall preference.

The natural outcome of this research approach has been to focus on changing preferences by identifying the important attributes associated with an object and trying to influence individuals' evaluations of the attributes. Nutrition educators often use this approach. They choose a food attribute, like dietary fiber, and tell people about its benefits. These educators believe that individuals will change their behavior, i.e., consumption of dietary fiber, if the individuals' evaluation of the attribute changes. Many nutrition educators, however, have learned from practical experience that this approach is not often successful. Zajonc and Markus's (1982) likely explanation for the lack of success in changing people's food preferences is that this approach assumes that cognition precedes the development of preferences, and that this may not be the case.

5

Most research reports of food-related behavior include at least a cursory description of the respondents' sociodemographic characteristics. Many include some examination of the relationship between the respondents' sociodemographic characteristics and their food-related behavior. This apparent concentration on sociodemographic characteristics to account for the observed variation in food-related behavior seems explained best by the relative ease in measuring these variables. Even though sociodemographic variables are often measured, the theoretical arguments for why these variables should be related to various measures of food-related behavior often are not given. This chapter differs from the others in this monograph in that the discussion of sociodemographic determinants focuses on the reasons why these characteristics might be related to food-related behavior and on the findings of studies rather than on the conceptualization and measurement of the variables. This approach is not meant to imply that there is not controversy surrounding the measurement of income or ethnicity, for example, but when compared to concepts like preferences, attitudes, or beliefs, the measurement of sociodemographic variables is rather straightforward. The sociodemographic determinants examined in this chapter include income, household size, education, gender, age, wife's employment status, and ethnicity.

Income

The functional relationship between income and food consumption (most often measured as monetary value of food consumed) is expressed by the Engel demand curve. According to Engel's law, when there is an increase in personal income, there is a decrease in the relative importance of the sum of money spent on food purchases as compared to other expenses, although an absolute increase in expenditure may result (Swagler, 1975). This relationship is usually expressed as either the marginal propensity to consume, which is defined as the change in food consumption resulting from a $1 increase in household income, or income elasticity, which is defined as the percentage change in food consumption resulting from a 1% change in income (Popkin and Haines, 1981). For food in the United States (US), the marginal propensity to consume or the income elasticity is very low (inelastic). Estimates of income elasticity for total food expenditures range from 0.17 (Price, 1982) to 0.36 (Salathe, 1979), which means that a 1% increase in household income produces a 0.17 to 0.36% increase in food expenditures. Thus, the relationship between income and food expenditures is not strong. The reason generally given is that food in the US is plentiful and relatively cheap compared to other countries.

Income elasticities also have been estimated for at-home and away-from-home food expenditures. An estimate of income elasticity for away-from-home food purchases is about 0.80 compared to 0.15 for at-home food purchases (Salathe, 1979; Smallwood and Blaylock, 1981). Findings from the US Department of Agriculture's 1977-1978 Nationwide Food Consumption Survey (NFCS) illustrate this point (Rizek and Peterkin, 1979). Low-income households (below $5000) spent approximately 14% of their food dollar for food away from home, whereas high-income households ($20,000 or more) spent 29% of their food dollar on food away from home. High-income households spent approximately five times more on food away from home than the low-income households.

Most foods have income elasticities of less than 0.50. The foods that are considered staples like milk, bread, and eggs have extremely low income elasticities (values approach zero), but meats and fresh fruits and vegetables are generally considered to have higher income elasticities (Popkin and Haines, 1981). More specifically, the food group containing meat, poultry, and fish had an estimated income elasticity of about 0.25, fruits 0.25, vegetables 0.17, and milk products 0.16. In comparison, eggs' and cereal products' elasticities were close to zero, fresh milk 0.08, and bread 0.04 (Abdel-Ghany and Schrimper, 1978; Salathe, 1979; Smallwood and Blaylock, 1981). Using the 1972-1973 Consumer Expenditure Survey, Blanciforti, Green, and Lane (1981) calculated income elasticities for relatively more nutritious foods and relatively less nutritious foods and found them to be equal.

The food usage pattern by income of individuals participating in the 1977-1978 NFCS was examined by Cronin and coworkers (1982). Food usage was defined as percentage of persons who reported using a food over a 3-day period. The pattern of food usage by income seems to reflect the pattern of the foods' income elasticities. Income was positively related to the usage of noncitrus fruits and "other" vegetables; cheese; meat, fish, and poultry; nuts; dessert, snack foods, and candy; and fats and salad dressings, whereas use of dried beans and peas, rice, and eggs was inversely related to income. Two other food items related positively to income were low-fat milk and whole-grain bread usage: these items probably are not related to income *per se*, but may reflect a growing concern about health in higher socioeconomic groups.

Compared to the income-food expenditure relationship, less work has been done on the income-nutrient intake and food expenditure-nutrient intake relationships (Davis, 1982). In analyzing data from the 1965-1966 NFCS, Adrian and Daniel (1976) found all nutrients except carbohydrate significantly and positively related to disposable income. Windham and associates (1983), however, did not find income related to the nutrient density (amount of nutrient/1000 kcal) of individuals' diets in the 1977-1978 NFCS. This finding may reflect measurement issues associated with using nutrient density as the criterion variable instead of using an indicator of dietary quality. Peterkin, Kerr, and Hama (1982) examined over 4000 low-income households that took part in the 1977-1978 NFCS and found that the nutritional quality of the diets, as measured by the percentage of diets meeting the Recommended Dietary Allowances, increased as food costs increased. Higher incomes or food expenditures do not necessarily result in an adequate diet. Nevertheless, as personal income increases, the possibility of adequate nutrient intakes seems to increase.

Household Size

Economists have observed that given the same income, larger households spend more on food than smaller households, but the value of the food purchased per person decreases with increasing household size. To assess the impact of household size on food expenditures, household size elasticities can be estimated. Household size elasticity (like income elasticity) is defined as the percentage change in food expenditures resulting from a 1% change in household size. Thus, a household size elasticity of more than 1.0 would indicate that a greater than 1% increase in food expenditure would result, and an elasticity of less than 1.0 means that a 1% increase in household size would result in less than a 1% increase in food expenditures (Smallwood and Blaylock, 1981). Because an increase in household size, given the same income, is in effect a decrease in income, an inverse relationship between income and household elasticities would be expected; that is, food items that are not responsive to income would be more responsive to changes in household size. Conversely, food products that are more responsive to income would have lower household size elasticities.

Using data from 1977-1978 NFCS, Smallwood and Blaylock (1981) examined food spending patterns by calculating both income and household size elasticities. For total food expenditures, income and household size elasticities were 0.32 and 0.57, respectively, which means that the addition of members to a household will cause a greater increase in food expenditures than will an increase in income. Household size elasticities for food at home and away from home were 0.73 and 0.11, respectively, whereas the income elasticities for food at home and away from home were 0.15 and 0.81, respectively. As expected, there was an inverse relationship between income and household size elasticities.

The food products most responsive to household size were fresh milk (household elasticity of 1.04) and dairy products (0.85); cereal products (1.10), bakery products (0.84), and bread (0.87); sugar products (1.00); potatoes (0.96); fats and oils (0.77), and eggs (0.75). Lower household size elasticities were estimated for fresh fruits (0.53), fresh vegetables (0.45), and juices (0.52). Although meats would be expected to have a relatively low household size elasticity because of its relatively high income elasticity, this was not the case. The household elasticities for beef (0.70) and poultry and fish (0.60) were higher than would be expected from their income elasticities-- 0.23 for beef and 0.17 for poultry and fish. In comparison, income elasticity for fresh vegetables was 0.18, with a household size elasticity of 0.45.

Windham and coworkers (1983) found household size to be significantly related to the nutrient density (amount of nutrient/1000 kcal) of individuals' diets. They found that households with 5+ members had a significantly lower nutrient density consumption of fat, but the mean difference was only 2 g/1000 kcal; households with 3+ members had a significantly higher nutrient density consumption of carbohydrate. These results correspond to the general pattern of the cereal products, sugar products, potatoes, bakery products, and breads having greater household size elasticities than fats and oils and meat. They also found vitamin C nutrient density consumption to be significantly and inversely related to household size, which corresponds to the lower household size elasticities of fresh fruits and vegetables. Vitamin B_6 was inversely related to household size, but vitamin B_6 is difficult to interpret because information on its content in foods and knowledge of bioavailability is limited.

Education

Investigators have included level of formal education as a predictor variable when examining some aspects of food-related behavior. Depending on the study, the educational level of the individual, male head of household, or female head of household is examined. Using household data from the 1965-1966 NFCS, Abdel-Ghany and Schrimper (1978) found that the educational level of the female head of household was positively related to total food expenditure in addition to expenditures for four out of nine food groups, even after accounting for income and other pertinent factors. Their calculated education elasticity was 0.12, compared to an income elasticity of 0.23. The education elasticities for fruits (0.32) and milk equivalents (0.18) were actually larger than their income elasticities, 0.25 and 0.11, respectively. The vegetable group and the meat, fish, and poultry group had education elasticities of 0.11 and 0.07, respectively. Using data from the 1972-1973 Consumer Expenditure Survey, however, Abdel-Ghany and Foster (1982) did not find a significant education elasticity (0.02). Both Adrian and Daniel (1976), using the 1965-1966 NFCS, and Windham and coworkers (1983), using the 1977-1978 NFCS, found the female head of household's educational level to be positively related to vitamin C consumption, which corresponds to the higher educational elasticity for fruit expenditures (Abdel-Ghany and Schrimper, 1978).

A number of investigators (e.g., Axelson, 1977; Caliendo and Sanjur, 1978; Eppright, Fox, Fryer, Lamkin, and Vivian, 1970; Schorr, Sanjur, and Erickson, 1972; Yperman and Vermeersch, 1979) have examined the relationship of mothers' (and sometimes fathers') educational levels to dietary quality, and they generally have found a positive, significant relationship. In addition, others (e.g., Schafer, Reger, Gillespie, and Roderuck, 1980; Sims, 1978) have found positive relationships (or trends) between women's educational levels and their dietary intake.

Although investigators have used educational level to predict food consumption and dietary quality, they often do not state explicitly how or why it should be related. Abdel-Ghany and Schrimper (1978) hypothesized that the educational level of the female head of household may be related to food consumption patterns for three reasons: the educational experience may increase productive capabilities by increasing household-related knowledge and skills, may increase nutrition knowledge or at least a general concern for health, and may affect preferences and general life-style. Educational level has been found to be related to nutrition knowledge by a number of investigators (e.g., Eppright, Fox, Fryer, Lamkin, and Vivian, 1970; Phillips, Bass, and Yetley, 1978; Sims, 1978; Woolcott, Kawash, and Sabry, 1981; Yetley and Roderuck, 1980), with reported zero-order correlation coefficients ranging from 0.25 to 0.63. In addition, level of formal education has been found to be inversely related to the use of convenience foods (Redman, 1980; Reilly, 1982), directly related to the number of meals that a household eats together (Ortiz, MacDonald, Ackerman, and Goebel, 1981), but not related to the number of meals eaten away from home (Ortiz, MacDonald, Ackerman, and Goebel, 1981; Redman, 1980).

Gender and Age

Gender and age are physiological states that may influence individuals' food consumption patterns. Cultures also may ascribe food patterns based on these physiological states. Consequently, the difficulty in examining differences between males and females of various ages is separating the physiological from the cultural effects.

Cronin and associates (1982) found few differences in food usage between males and females participating in the 1977-1978 NFCS. For 54 out of 65 food groups examined, they found no difference in food usage. Of the remaining food groups, a greater percentage of women than men reported using citrus fruits, yogurt, coffee and tea, and low-calorie carbonated beverages in a 3-day period. A greater percentage of men reported using whole milk; luncheon meats; meat, fish, and poultry sandwiches; desserts, sugar, and sweet spreads. These differences, however, were not dramatic. The largest difference was in the use of luncheon meat, with 61% of the men versus 51% of the women reporting its use. These investigators also calculated the mean number of times per day that the foods were used by the individuals who reported using the food. Means between males and females did not differ for 21 out of 32 food groups, but females did report using foods in 11 groups fewer times per day. These food groups included breads and cereals; milk, yogurt, and cheese; meat, fish, poultry, and eggs; desserts, sugar, and sweet spreads.

Differences in food preferences (degree of liking) between males and females have been reported (e.g., Einstein and Hornstein, 1970; Logue and Smith, 1986; Wyant and Meiselman, 1984). For example, a consistent finding is that women more than men prefer fruits and vegetables. One explanation for these differences in food preferences is that adoption of a particular food consumption pattern causes a greater exposure to particular foods, which then may enhance the preferences for them. The reason for the adoption of a particular food consumption pattern may be physiological (e.g., generally, women need to consume less energy, thus, choose more low-calorie foods) or social (e.g., women are taught to eat salads because salads are considered more "feminine"). There appears to be no evidence to support or reject either of these explanations. Logue and Smith (1986) found significant differences between female and male preferences for approximately one-third of the foods they studied, although they note that the differences were never greater than one point on a 9-point, like/dislike scale. This observation caused Logue and Smith (1986, pg 114) to conclude that "significant sex differences in food preferences . . . may be unnoticeable in daily life."

Because women are usually smaller and have less lean body mass than men, they need less energy; consequently, they eat less than men. As a result of the lower energy needs, the food consumption patterns of women may differ from men in three general ways:

women may eat the same variety of foods but in smaller amounts than men, or they may eat a smaller variety of foods but in the same amounts, or they may show a combination of the two strategies. Even though Cronin *et al.* (1982) present data based on food usage and not food quantities consumed, the results still seem to indicate that women may be using the strategy of eating the same variety of foods as men, but in smaller amounts.

Most studies that consider age have cross-sectional research designs or just examine a particular age group at one point in time (teenagers and the elderly are especially popular). This type of study does not allow the partitioning of the effect due to aging or the effect due to cohort. As Garcia, Battese, and Brewer (1975, pg 349) point out, differences in food-related behavior among cohorts may come about because of technological, economic, and social changes in a society, and "any effects of generational patterns of eating must be accounted for if valid inferences are to be made as to the effects of aging *per se* on dietary intakes."

A few longitudinal studies (Garcia, Battese, and Brewer, 1975; Ohlson and Harper, 1976; Steinkamp, Cohen, and Walsh, 1965) have been reported. Garcia and coworkers (1975) followed 35 women, born between 1873 and 1931, over an 18-year period. Four dietary intake measurements were collected between 1948 and 1969. Using multiple regression, they estimated the effects of cohort and aging on nutrient intake. With increasing age, the women reduced significantly their fat intake and increased significantly their calcium intake. There also was a downward trend ($p < 0.10$) in energy intake due to age. The cohort effect accounted for more of the variation in nutrient intake among the women. The younger the cohort, the higher the intakes of protein, calcium, phosphorus, iron, riboflavin, and niacin. Intakes of carbohydrate, thiamin, vitamin A, and ascorbic acid were not related to either cohort or age effects. These authors concluded that nutrient intakes do not change significantly from middle to old age. Investigators (Ohlson and Harper, 1976; Steinkamp, Cohen, and Walsh, 1965) of other longitudinal studies reported similar results, in that a general decrease in food energy was observed with age, but not any dramatic changes in food consumption patterns; unfortunately, their lack of statistical analyses precludes more specific comment.

Windham and associates (1981) compared the nutrient densities (amount of nutrient/1000 kcal) of foods consumed by various sex-age groups. Comparing nutrient density rather than absolute amounts of nutrients corrects for the differences in energy needs due to gender or age. Using the 1977-1978 NFCS data, these investigators found that the nutrient densities of diets did not differ between males and females, with the exception that females consumed diets that contained more vitamin A and vitamin C per 1000 kcal than males. They also found no dramatic differences among age groups (range 4 to 65+), with again the exceptions of vitamins A and C. The younger and older age groups had diets more dense in these nutrients.

In our culture, there seem to be virtually no dietary proscriptions based on gender or age; thus, physiologically-based rather than culturally-based reasons are more likely to explain most of the variance found in food consumption patterns between males and females within a cohort. On the other hand, differences found among age groups (cohorts) in food consumption patterns, after correcting for energy needs, seem to be more culturally based.

Wife's Employment Status

Women in our culture perform most of the housework. Food-related activities like meal preparation are still the domain of women and account for a large proportion of time spent in housework (Waite, 1981). Because of the dramatic increase in women's employment outside the home, especially of married women with young children (Waite, 1981), investigators have turned their attention to studying the effect of wives' employment on households' food production and consumption. Contrary to the perception that husbands and wives are sharing more household-related tasks as a result of the changing sex roles in our society, working wives still perform most of the housework. In fact, Waite (1981) reports that the hours spent in housework by working wives was six times greater than the hours spent by married men. Consequently, research has focused on the strategies used by working wives to satisfy the competing demands of their jobs and households.

Investigators (Hafstrom and Schram, 1983; Nickols and Fox, 1983; Nickols and Metzen, 1978; Stafford, 1983) have found that as the number of wives' employment hours increases, the number of hours they spend in housework decreases. More specifically, the more hours wives spent employed outside the home, the fewer hours they spent in meal preparation, with estimates of about 15-20 minutes per day less for employed wives compared to unemployed wives (Goebel and Hennon, 1982, 1983; Ortiz, MacDonald, Ackerman, and Goebel, 1981). This inverse relationship between employment time and meal preparation time has generated speculation and investigation as to the means by which working wives decrease their meal preparation time.

Collective wisdom has attributed some of the increase in away-from-home food consumption in the US to the increased employment of women outside the home because purchasing meals would be an obvious way to decrease housework time. Investigators (Goebel and Hennon, 1982, 1983; Lippert and Love, 1986), controlling for income, have found no relationship between wives' employment status (e.g., part time, full time) and expenditures for meals away from home. Goebel and Hennon (1982) did find, however, a significant but low, positive correlation ($r = 0.14$) between number of hours employed and expenditures for food away from home. Ortiz *et al.* (1981) found that the percentage of meals eaten away from home by households increased significantly when the female head of household worked full time (30 hr. or more per week), but not when she worked part time. Similarly, hours of wives' employment were directly related to eating at fast-food establishments and school cafeterias, but not eating at other types of restaurants (Nickols and Fox, 1983). The inconsistencies in findings are probably related to differences in the operationalization of the variables under study (e.g., hours of employment versus employment status). There does seem to be a trend for households with employed wives to eat more meals away from home; however, as Goebel and Hennon (1982, pg 75) comment, there is probably "no substantial substitution of money for time in the sense of purchasing meals away from home."

Another strategy women may use to decrease meal preparation time is to increase their use of convenience foods. Havlicek and coworkers (1983), Lippert and Love (1986), and Redman (1980), using national surveys, found employment of wives (or of primary meal planners) to be positively and significantly related to use of convenience foods. When examining use of convenience foods by about 200 households in Wisconsin, Reilly (1982) did not find a relationship between convenience food use and wives' employment status. A problem with studying convenience food use is the ambiguity in the definition of convenience foods. Reilly (1982) seems to have used a more restricted definition (smaller number of foods) than Havlicek *et al.* (1983) and Redman (1980).

Wives' employment also has not been found to be related to food preparation style (as measured by number of food items per meal, difficulty of food preparation, frequency of preparing food ahead) (Nickols and Fox, 1983) or to the number of meals eaten together by the household (Goebel and Hennon, 1983; Ortiz, MacDonald, Ackerman, and Goebel, 1981). These factors seem to be more related to age of the children in the household. In addition, the nutrition implications of wives' employment status have been investigated (Skinner, Ezell, Salvetti, and Penfield, 1985; Windham, Wyse, Hurst, and Hansen, 1983), and there appears to be no relationship between nutrient intakes of household members and female head of household's employment status.

Ethnicity and Race

The literature related to cultural subgroups in the US can be divided according to the primary question that is addressed. There seem to be three basic questions: 1) What are the foodways of a particular ethnic group in the US? 2) How does a particular ethnic group's foodways in the US differ from the group's foodways in their culture of origin? 3) How does a particular ethnic group differ from the dominant cultural group?

Descriptions of cultural subgroups in the US dominate the literature. The method of examining one group at one point in time, however, has limitations. The food-related practices described are attributed either implicitly or explicitly to ethnicity, which may not be the case because alternative explanations (like income and geographic region) cannot be rejected. At the least, when studying ethnicity as a determinant of behavior, the ethnic group should be compared to a dominant cultural group that is similar in socioeconomic status and lives in the same geographic area. Even though these descriptive studies of only one ethnic group contribute little to the understanding of ethnicity as a determinant of food- related behavior, they can provide, if current, useful information to health practitioners in the field working with particular cultural subgroups. Because the US has so many ethnic groups, descriptions of each are not addressed.

When individuals immigrate to the US, what impact does the American culture have on their food-related behavior? The measured degree of cultural impact depends greatly on the level of analysis (e.g., food preparation methods, meal patterns, or foods consumed). To assess changes in the types and amounts of foods consumer, Dewey, Strode, and Fitch (1984) provide a tripartite food categorization system: *traditional* foods--those that are more common in the culture of origin; *basic* foods--those that are common to both cultures; and *new* foods--those that are more common in the host culture.

Using this food categorization system, Dewey *et al.* (1984) examined the degree of acculturation of two groups (nonmigrants and migrants) of low-income, first-generation Mexican Americans. The food-use frequency of 54 foods was assessed. They found that even though both groups reported an increased use of both basic and new foods, the nonmigrants' (or more permanent groups') use of these foods was significantly greater than the migrants. The nonmigrants and migrants, however, were similar in their decreased use of traditional foods. Controlling for income and household size, Wallendorf and Reilly (1983) examined the consumption of basic foods of urban Mexican Americans and urban Mexicans. They found that Mexican Americans ate fewer eggs but more meat, white bread, cereals, soft drinks, and caffeine-containing beverages than their counterparts in Mexico. The Mexican Americans continued using tortillas, but used more pre-prepared ones than did the Mexicans. Pattern of alcohol consumption differed, with Mexican Americans drinking more beer and wine and Mexicans more spirits.

The nutrient intakes of Puerto-Rico-born females who lived in Puerto Rico (nonmigrants), lived in the US (forward migrants), and lived in Puerto Rico after living in the US (return migrants) were compared (Immink, Sanjur, and Burgos, 1983). Even after controlling for socioeconomic variables, the forward migrants had better nutrient intakes than either the nonmigrants or return migrants. The authors also observed that the women who returned to Puerto Rico resumed their customary Puerto Rican diets.

First-generation Chinese Americans were asked about their food consumption of traditional and nontraditional foods available in the US when living in China and after living in the US (Grivetti and Paquette, 1978; Yang and Fox, 1979). Results, which were similar to the studies of Spanish-speaking populations, indicated a decreased use of traditional foods, even though they were available, and an increased use of basic and new foods. This trend also was identified by Tong (1986) in Vietnamese who had immigrated to the US and by Jerome (1980) in Blacks who had migrated from the southern to northern part of the US. At a different level of analysis, however, acculturation is not evident. The food-related beliefs about appropriate foods for the elderly did not differ between Chinese and first-generation Chinese Americans (Newman and Ludman, 1984). On the other hand, Freedman and Grivetti (1984) found that the abandonment of traditional beliefs associated with diet and pregnancy was fairly complete by the third generation in a group of Greek American women.

These studies indicate that food-related behavior is modified by culture, and many of the observed changes in the amounts and types of foods consumed cannot be explained by availability of the foods or by change in socioeconomic status of the individuals. Although the types of foods consumed may change, some investigators (Jerome, 1980; Yang and Fox, 1979) have observed that the characteristic food preparation methods of the culture of origin often are retained.

Do ethnic groups differ in their food-related behaviors from the dominant cultural group? Even though answers to this question are important to investigators of food-related behavior as well as to food and nutrition policy makers, there is a paucity of empirical research. Nevertheless, results of investigations that have controlled for sociodemographic variables indicate that there are differences between cultural subgroups and dominant cultural groups (e.g., Caster, 1980; Netland and Brownstein, 1984; Salathe, Gallo, and Boehm, 1979; Wallendorf and Reilly, 1983; Windham, Wyse, Hansen, and Hurst, 1983).

According to data from the 1972-1974 Consumer Expenditure Survey, when compared to whites, blacks purchased more beef, pork, poultry, fish, and seafood, but less cereal and bakery products, sugary products, dairy products, and nonalcoholic beverages (Salathe, Gallo and Boehm, 1979). Other investigators (Brittin and Zinn, 1977) also have reported more meat purchases by blacks than whites. Rozin and Cines (1982) found less use of coffee among blacks compared to whites and attributed the differences to socialization. Caster (1980) compared low-income black and white women living in the same geographic region on their food-use frequency of 150 foods in 3 groups--core diet (24% of the foods, which provided 69% of the diets' energy), secondary diet (33% foods and 27% energy), and peripheral diet (43% foods and 4% energy). The two groups did not differ in their core diets, but differences were found in their secondary diets. Because the peripheral diet was considered to be of little nutritional consequence, it was not analyzed.

Comparing Mexican American and Anglos (researchers' term), Wallendorf and Reilly (1983) found that the Mexican Americans consumed more eggs, white bread, and tortillas and less dry cereals, pastries, wine, and beer than the Anglos, but the two groups consumed the same amount of convenience foods, soft drinks, and coffee and tea. They concluded that the Mexican Americans' consumption patterns were not like their culture of origin or their culture of residence. In fact, they felt that the Mexican American patterns were reminiscent of stereotypical American patterns of consumption before the widespread interest in food and health.

The nutrient density of calcium was found to be greater in the diets of whites than of either blacks or Spanish-speaking individuals. The nutrient density of vitamin A also differed among the groups, with blacks having diets that were the most dense and Spanish-speaking individuals the least dense. Asians were found to have diets higher in carbohydrate, but lower in fat, vitamin A, riboflavin, and calcium than whites (Netland and Brownstein, 1984).

Cultural subgroups seem to exhibit food-related behavior unlike their culture of origin as well as unlike their culture of residence. Ethnicity seems to be a significant predictor of food-related behavior; however, this determinant probably becomes a poorer predictor for descending generations of immigrants. When social barriers are removed, access to the dominant culture is allowed.

6

Numerous models have been proposed to examine the relationships among beliefs, attitudes, and behavior. These models, which are called decision making or choice models, focus on behaviors that are under the volitional control of the individual; that is, behaviors that are determined by individuals' conscious beliefs and attitudes and not determined by habitual (or unconscious) processes. All these models incorporate constructs that allow for individual and social influences; however, the manner in which these constructs are defined and measured varies.

Two types of models--nomothetic and idiographic--are examined in this chapter. Nomothetic models attempt to develop generalizable rules of choice behavior that apply across individuals. The nomothetic models presented in this chapter are Fishbein and Ajzen's Theory of Reasoned Action, Triandis's Theory of Social Behavior, and a subjective probability model. Idiographic models attempt to determine the decision processes used by the individual. The idiographic models presented in this chapter are social judgment theory and a behavioral alternatives model.

Fishbein and Ajzen's Theory of Reasoned Action

Fishbein and Ajzen's (1975) definitions of beliefs, attitudes, and intentions were used in Chapter 3 to examine these constructs and to compare the expectancy-value and the tripartite views of attitudes. Beliefs, attitudes, and intentions, however, are important only if they can be used to predict people's behavior. Since Fishbein and

Ajzen (1975) published their social-psychological theory of decision making, it has been applied to a wide variety of behaviors, including some food-related behaviors. Before examining the findings from these studies, a brief description of the theory is given first.

Fishbein and Ajzen (1975) hypothesize that an individual's intention to perform some behavior is the best predictor of that behavior. Even though individuals' intentions generally predict their behavior, only through the identification of the determinants of their intentions does an understanding of the reasons for their behavior occur. According to this theory, intention is a function of an individual's attitude toward performing the behavior, or act, plus the effect that significant others have on the individual's performance of the behavior, i.e., the subjective norm. Fishbein and Ajzen describe the relationships among the components of the model in the following manner:

$$\text{Behavior} \simeq \text{Intention} = \text{Attitude } (w_1) + \text{Subjective Norm } (w_2). \quad (6\text{-}1)$$

The parameters, w_1 and w_2, reflect the relative importance of attitude and subjective norm, respectively, in determining intention. Investigators usually determine these parameters, or weights, by regression analysis. The influence of external variables such as income, gender, age, and personality traits on a particular behavior is assumed to be mediated through the components of the model.

Attitude refers to "a learned predisposition to respond in a consistently favorable or unfavorable manner toward some object or act" (Fishbein and Ajzen, 1975, pg 6) and is determined by the sum of the individual's salient beliefs (b_i) about the consequences of performing the behavior multiplied by the individual's evaluation (e_i) of those consequences. Fishbein and Ajzen express this relationship as follows:

$$\text{Attitude}_{(act)} = \Sigma\, b_i e_i. \quad (6\text{-}2)$$

The subjective norm refers to the individual's perception of what important others think the individual should do and is determined by the sum of the individual's normative beliefs (Nb), that is, beliefs concerning what important others think about the individual's performing the particular behavior multiplied by the individual's motivation to comply with the wishes of those significant others (Mc). Fishbein and Ajzen express this relationship as follows:

$$\text{Subjective Norm} = \Sigma \, NbMc. \tag{6-3}$$

Equation 6-1 indicates that Fishbein and Ajzen's model for understanding and predicting behavior contains two aspects. First, these authors believe that the best predictor of behavior is an individual's intention. On some levels, this relationship is quite trivial. If a researcher is interested in whether some people will eat dinner at a particular restaurant, and these people are asked their intentions to eat at that restaurant at dinner time when they are outside the restaurant, their intentions will be a very strong predictor of their behavior. If prediction is the sole criterion for evaluating the utility of the model, then the model would be judged as quite successful.

The second major aspect of the model is the prediction of a person's intention. Fishbein and Ajzen (1975) maintain that attitude toward the act and subjective norm are the necessary and sufficient predictors of intention. That is, the variables external to the model (such as personality, age, gender, and values) influence intention only through their impact on beliefs, attitude, and/or subjective norm. The prediction of intention is somewhat trivial when using attitude and subjective norm as the determinants of intention. Simply described, the model states that an individual is likely to perform a behavior if he (she) thinks that the behavior is good and if people who are important to him (her) think that the behavior should be performed. Like the intention-behavior relationship, if prediction is the goal of the research, then the model is likely to be judged as adequate. If changing intention and behavior is the focus of the research, however, then the model becomes meaningful only when the researcher can identify the determinants of intention; that is, the information provided in equations 6-2 and 6-3.

Predicting Behavior. Fishbein and Ajzen (1975) describe a number of parameters that researchers need to address when predicting a person's behavior--target, time, context, and action. Target refers to the object at which the behavior is directed, time refers to when the behavior is to be performed, context refers to a particular location in which the behavior will occur, and action refers to the type of behavior to be performed. For example, Mary may take Joe (target) to dinner (action) tonight (time) at the Thai Room (context). Each of these parameters varies along a dimension of specificity. For instance, a researcher may ask an individual his (her) intention to eat a particular food (like grits), but not specify the time period within which the behavior can occur (e.g., the next six months). The constructs in the Theory of Reasoned Action, according to Fishbein and Ajzen (1975), will be related only if they correspond in their level of specificity. That is, the constructs of the model (beliefs, attitude, subjective norm, intention, and behavior) should correspond with respect to time, target, context, and action. If these constructs do not correspond, then the researcher should not expect to find significant relations among the constructs of the model (e.g., between intention and behavior). Suppose that you were interested in predicting a person's eating behavior at a specific fast-food restaurant (such as Wendy's in East Schodack) during a specific time period (e.g., February 4th and 5th). If you ask an individual his or her intention to eat at fast-food restaurants in general, then this individual may indicate a strong positive intention to eat at these restaurants. But, when you measure a specific behavior (e.g., eating at Wendy's in East Schodack on the weekend of February 4th), you probably will find that the individual did not eat at the restaurant. One inference that might be drawn from this finding is that intention does not predict behavior. A more reasonable inference, however, is that a relationship between intention and behavior would not occur because the measures of behavior and intention do not correspond in terms of time, target, context, and action. If the researcher obtains a general measure of intention, such as the intention to eat at fast-food restaurants, then the measure of behavior should be general--that is, a successful behavioral performance of the intention should be the eating at <u>any</u> fast-food restaurant during <u>any</u> time period.

As a practical matter, the level of specificity of these parameters may be determined by first starting with the behavior of interest. When the parameters for the behavior are determined, the researcher then is able to determine the level of each parameter for each construct in the model.

Besides the level of specificity of these parameters, several other factors affect the intention-behavior relationship. The amount of time between the measure of intention and the actual performance of the behavior has been found to affect the intention-behavior relationship. Specifically, the greater the amount of time between the measures of intention and behavior, the weaker the relationship between these two variables. One explanation for this observation is that the individual may obtain new information between the time his or her intention was measured and the actual occurrence of the behavior. This new information may cause a change in the individual's intention, which may affect the performance of the behavior. Another factor is the number of additional behaviors that need to occur prior to the occurrence of the target behavior. For example, suppose that the target behavior is consuming five servings of vegetables per day and that an individual states that his or her intention is to meet this goal. For the individual to complete the behavior successfully, several other behaviors must occur first. The individual must go to the store to purchase the food, must have the resources to make this purchase, and must have the food available at the store to make the purchase. Failure to complete any of these behaviors would result in a failure to perform the target behavior. In a similar manner, if the performance of the behavior is contingent on the action of another

individual or an external event, then the relationship between someone's intention and behavior may be affected. A child, for example,
may learn in school about the importance of eating green, leafy
vegetables and may state an intention to eat them at least three times
a week. If the meal preparer of the child's household does not share
this intention, however, then the child will not perform the behavior.

The habit, ability, and knowledge of a person may cause an
attenuation of the intention-behavior relationship. Several
researchers (e.g., Triandis, 1977) have found that habitual behavior
may affect the relationship between intention and behavior. Suppose
that an individual is "in the habit" of eating a particular breakfast
cereal. He or she goes to the store with the intention to purchase a
new, high-fiber cereal. At the store, however, the individual becomes
distracted (e.g., by point-of-purchase advertising) and "inadvertently"
purchases the familiar brand. In this case, the habit, rather than the
individual's intention, was the best predictor of the behavior. For
those behaviors with a well-established behavioral pattern, habit (past
behavior) will often be a better predictor of behavior than intention.
Knowledge and ability refer to an individual's skills to perform a
behavior and the availability of adequate resources. For example, a
person decides (intends) to increase his or her intake of dietary fiber.
Intention, however, may not predict behavior if the individual does
not have an adequate knowledge of the dietary fiber content of
different foods. This individual may believe that lettuce is high in
fiber because it is crisp. Although the individual's intention is positive, the appropriate behavior will not occur because of his or her lack
of knowledge. As with knowledge, an individual may intend to
perform the behavior, but overestimates his or her ability to perform
the behavior. For example, if food high in fiber takes a lot of time to
prepare, then an individual may be unable to prepare the food
because of time constraints.

Fishbein and Ajzen (1975) argue that the effect of these
external variables (i.e., time, habit, additional information, ability, and
knowledge) on behavior will be mediated through intention. That is,

the person will modify his or her intention given changes in these external variables, and this modified intention will be sufficient to predict behavior. At this point in time, the empirical evidence concerning the sufficiency of intention as a predictor of behavior and the incremental contribution of these external factors on behavior is unresolved.

Predicting Intention. Individuals' attitude and subjective norm are determined by their salient beliefs (multiplied by the evaluation of those beliefs and the motivation to comply, respectively). Equations 6-2 and 6-3 depict the elements of attitude and subjective norm. Salience refers to a belief that is a determinant of attitude, which is usually identified by using an elicitation procedure that asks respondents to indicate the advantages and disadvantages of performing the behavior. The beliefs that are elicited most frequently are described as salient and treated as determinants of behavior.

The constructs that predict intention also provide a useful structure for examining the impact of changing any single belief on an individual's attitude, subjective norm, intention, and behavior. For example, suppose that a researcher is interested in increasing an individual's intake of dietary fiber. Let's assume that attitude (and not subjective norm) is the primary determinant of intention. Typically, this finding is determined through the use of regression analysis and the interpretation of the standardized regression coefficients associated with attitude and subjective norm. The specific beliefs to focus on in a change study (i.e., those beliefs most likely to affect attitude, intention, and the subsequent behavior) are identified by using the following strategy. First, the researcher separates the sample into two groups--those individuals who indicate a positive intention to perform the behavior (on the 7-point, likely/unlikely scale) and those individuals who indicate a negative intention to perform the behavior. Those individuals with a "neutral" intention are not included in this analysis. Second, these two groups--intenders and nonintenders--are compared with respect to their beliefs and the evaluations of these beliefs. Those items that differentiate intenders from nonintenders are treated as "target" beliefs and are the focus of educational (change) messages.

Although the researcher/educator may be successful in changing the target beliefs, behavior may not change for several reasons. First, a change in a belief does not require a subsequent change in attitude because the evaluation of the belief may change in a manner that compensates for the change in belief (i.e., there is no change in the overall sum of the beliefs times evaluations). To illustrate, suppose that the educator changes an individual's perception concerning the ease of obtaining food that is high in fiber from a rating of +1 to a rating of +2. But now because of the belief change, the evaluation of the belief also changes from a +2 to a +1. The overall score would remain unchanged--thus, no change in attitude or intention. Second, a change in one belief may have an impact on another belief such that the net change in the sum of the $b_i e_i$ products is zero--thus, no change in attitude or intention. Again, let's say that the educator changes an individual's perception concerning the taste of a food from +1 to +3, but this change also affects the perception of cost, which changes from +3 to +1. The overall change in the sum of the $b_i e_i$ products would be zero. If the overall $b_i e_i$ product changes, then attitude would be predicted to change. Intention may not necessarily change, however, because subjective norm may change in a manner that compensates for the change in attitude. And, even if intention changes, many factors may affect the occurrence of the behavior.

Limitations of the Model. Questions have been raised about how the model's components are structured and measured. First, one issue addresses the separation of the attitudinal and normative beliefs. Some researchers (e.g., Ryan, 1982) argue that there is no justification for the separation of these beliefs into two constructs and present evidence suggesting that the same set of beliefs affects both attitude and subjective norm. A second issue focuses on the integration rule used to combine the beliefs for both the attitude and subjective norm constructs (i.e., the summation of the products of beliefs x evaluations). This integration rule assumes that the beliefs are independent of each other and that the rule to combine these beliefs is additive. Both of these assumptions have been questioned. Jaccard and Wood (1986) present data indicating that beliefs are not independent of each other and that an additive integration rule does not always represent the process by which the information is combined. Third, the concept of salience also has created some problems in the application of the Theory of Reasoned Action. Because Fishbein and Ajzen (1975) do not provide a method for measuring salience other than the use of an open-ended elicitation procedure, the researcher is unable to determine whether the beliefs used in a study are the determinants of attitude; that is, whether the beliefs are salient or simply inferential beliefs that reflect an individual's attitude rather than determine it. Fourth, a methodological limitation in the analysis of the Fishbein and Ajzen model has been the interpretation of standardized regression coefficients as indices of importance. These coefficients are susceptible to several sources of disturbance (e.g., multicollinearity, different weights applied by each individual to the attitude and subjective norm constructs) and the use of these coefficients as indices of importance is suspect. Alternative strategies for measuring importance will be presented in our discussion of the subjective probability model, social judgment theory, and the behavioral alternatives model.

A final issue associated with the Fishbein and Ajzen model is the level of analysis at which the model is used. Purportedly, this model examines the decision process of an individual, but both the data collection and analytic procedures are nomothetic (designed to assess general laws) and do not allow the assessment of the decision process for any one individual. Jaccard and Dittus (in press) examine these issues in their presentation of idiographic (individual) versus nomothetic (aggregate level) models of decision making. These authors argue that nomothetic models fail to capture an individual's decision process because each individual may use the rating (response) scale differently so that aggregate-level analyses mask these differences. In other words, nomothetic analyses examine an individual's response relative to other individuals rather than in relationship to the individual's other perceptions/preferences. For example, regression/correlation techniques applied to Fishbein and Ajzen's model determine whether people who have positive attitudes relative to people who have negative attitudes are more likely to perform a behavior.

Applications of the Model in the Study of Food-Related Behavior. The Theory of Reasoned Action has received substantial attention in the social and behavioral sciences. Recently, food and nutrition researchers have applied this model to a variety of food-related behaviors. Table 6.1 contain a list of some of these studies and their major findings.

The correlations between intention and behavior in Table 6.1 all are significant ($p < 0.01$). This finding indicates that Fishbein and Ajzen's model is able to predict a variety of food-related behaviors. The attitude toward the act was a consistent predictor of intention (all the standardized regression coefficients were significant), and subjective norm was inconsistently related to intention (less than half of the standardized regression coefficients were statistically significant).

Several studies which used components of the Fishbein and Ajzen model were excluded from Table 6-1 because they did not provide a direct test of the model. These studies, however, do provide indirect support for the Fishbein and Ajzen model. Feldman and Mayhew (1984) used the model to predict the consumption of meat and sodium and found support for the intention-behavior relationship. These authors also found that past behavior (habit) and the ease or difficulty of performing the behavior (knowledge and ability) made significant, independent contributions to the prediction of behavior. They did not examine the intention component of the model. Tuorila-Ollilainen and coworkers (1987b) found that the inclusion of a hedonic measure (i.e., sensory-related affect) improved the amount of variance accounted for in intention ($\approx 14\%$). Cote, McCullough, and Reilly (1985) found that situational variables

Table 6.1

Application of Fishbein and Ajzen's Model to Food-Related Behavior

Authors	Type of Behavior	$BI - B$[a]	$I = \text{Att}(w_1) + \text{SN}(w_2)$[b]		
Manstead et al. (1983)	Breast-feeding	0.82^{**}	0.77^{**}	0.46^{**}	0.45^{**}
	Formula-feeding		0.77^{**}	0.53^{**}	0.19^{**}
Tuorila (1987b)	Consumption of Nonfat milk	0.64^{**}	0.59^{**}	0.55^{**}	0.09
	Low-fat milk	0.54^{**}	0.39^{**}	0.38^{**}	0.10
	Reg-fat milk	0.62^{**}	0.60^{**}	0.41^{**}	0.28^{**}
Shepherd & Stockley (1987)	Fat consumption	0.69^{**}	0.69^{**}	0.59^{**}	0.18
Tuorila-Ollilainen et al. (1986)	Low-salt bread consumption	0.55^{**}	0.44^{**}	0.35^{**}	0.23
Axelson, Brinberg & Durand (1983)	Eating at a fast-food restaurant	0.41^{**}	0.65^{**}	0.64^{**}	0.03

[a] BI refers to intention and B refers to behavior; correlation coefficients are listed in the first column.

[b] The values in these three columns represent 1) the multiple correlation of attitude and subjective norm with intention, 2) w_1, the standardized regression coefficient of attitude, and 3) w_2, the standardized regression coefficient of subjective norm.

[**] $p < 0.01$.

(e.g., guests visiting, weather) accounted for a significant percentage of the variance in behavior over and above the contribution of intention (and past behavior). These authors, however, did not report a test of the intention model or the zero-order correlations among the constructs of the model.

The results of these studies, collectively, provide substantial support for both aspects of the Fishbein and Ajzen model--the prediction of behavior and the prediction of intention. Several sets of empirical findings, however, suggest that the model does not provide the necessary and sufficient predictors of intention and behavior because other variables (such as past behavior, situational factors) contribute to the prediction of behavior and intention.

Triandis's Model of Social Behavior

Triandis (1977) proposed a model of social behavior to predict an individual's behavior and his or her intention to perform the behavior. This model may be expressed as follows:

$$\text{Behavior} = F * H (w_1) + F * I (w_2), \tag{6-4}$$

where F represents the facilitating conditions, defined as the ease or difficulty of performing the behavior, the person's knowledge about the behavior, and the person's motivation to perform the behavior; H represents habit, defined as the number of times the behavior has been performed in the past; I represents intention, defined as the individual's perceived likelihood of performing a behavior, and w_1 and w_2 represent theoretical parameters which reflect the relative importance of habit and intention, respectively, in predicting behavior.

Triandis proposed the following model to predict an individual's intention:

$$\text{Intention} = \text{affect} (w_3) + \text{consequences} (w_4) + \text{social determinants}(w_5), \tag{6-5}$$

where affect represents the emotional response associated with the behavior; consequences represent the sum of the beliefs associated with the behavior multiplied by the evaluation of those beliefs (i.e., $\Sigma b_i e_i$); social determinants represent norms, roles, moral norm and self-concept, and w_3, w_4, and w_5 represent theoretical parameters which reflect the relative importance of each construct in predicting intention. A norm, according to Triandis (1977), is the appropriateness of the behavior for a particular group of people. For example, an individual may be asked whether she considers herself to be a member of a particular group (e.g., the American Dietetics Association) and then asked whether it is appropriate for individuals who belong to ADA to perform a particular behavior (e.g., eat dinner at fast-food restaurants). Triandis (1977) believes that roles also address the issue of the appropriateness of the behavior, but that they focus on the individual's position in a social system. For example, motherhood holds a particular position in our society and some behaviors may be appropriate for a woman in her role as mother (e.g., prepare healthful foods for her family), which may not be appropriate for her when she hosts a cocktail party. Moral norm refers to an individual's perceived moral obligation to perform a behavior. For example, many parents tell their children that they should finish the food on their plate because "there are people starving in [insert country]." This type of statement calls on a perceived moral obligation not to waste food. Lastly, self-concept refers to the attributes that an individual associates with himself or herself--such as healthy, slim, and athletic.

Comparison of the Triandis and Fishbein-Ajzen Models. Similar to Fishbein and Ajzen's model, Triandis's model contains two major aspects--the prediction of behavior and the prediction of intention. In the Triandis model, behavior is determined by habit, intention, and facilitating conditions. In contrast, the Fishbein and Ajzen model views intention as the best predictor of behavior, although these authors acknowledge that the intention-behavior relationship is an approximation. Whereas Fishbein and Ajzen describe factors that may influence the intention-behavior relationship, Triandis's model incorporates several factors explicitly. According to Triandis (1977), facilitating conditions should be scored on a scale ranging from 0 (behavior is very difficult, and the person has no knowledge) to 1 (behavior is very easy, and the person is very knowledgeable). An important implication of the multiplicative relationship between facilitating conditions, habit, and intention is that when facilitating conditions are 0, then the behavior will not be performed, even if the person has performed the behavior in the past and intends to perform the behavior in the future. For example, suppose that Steve intends to purchase Ben & Jerry's ice cream and regularly purchases this brand of ice cream twice a week. If the store does not have the ice cream (thus making the behavior impossible), then the purchase behavior will not occur even though Steve's intention is positive and he has performed the behavior in the past.

In the prediction of intention, the Fishbein and Ajzen model and the Triandis model have substantial similarities and differences. Both models include an expectancy-value construct. Fishbein and Ajzen label this construct attitude, whereas Triandis labels it consequences. These constructs, however, are the same conceptually and operationally. Therefore, the limitations discussed with respect to the attitude concept in Fishbein and Ajzen's model are applicable to the consequence construct in Triandis's model.

Both models include an estimate of social pressure, but do so in different ways. Fishbein and Ajzen focus on what specific, relevant others believe that the individual should do and measure the individual's motivation to comply with those significant others. Triandis, on the other hand, focuses on a more general measure of social pressure; that is, the appropriateness of a behavior for a group to which the individual belongs and for his or her role. In addition to appropriateness of the behavior, Triandis includes moral norm and self-concept.

Both models measure affect (evaluation), but measure them in different ways. Fishbein and Ajzen measure affect by assessing the individual's attitude toward performing the behavior. Triandis separates affect (emotional response) from consequences (i.e., an attitude from the Fishbein-Ajzen perspective) and argues that each construct can make a separate, independent contribution toward the prediction of intention. For example, both affect and consequences might contribute to an individual's intention to eat candy. The affective response is likely to be positive and the consequences are likely to be negative; thus, either (or both) factor(s) may influence the intention. Fishbein and Ajzen argue that measuring both affect and consequences is redundant because both constructs measure an individual's attitude. Some empirical evidence (e.g., Brinberg, 1979; Tuorila, 1987b) suggests that affect and attitude are separable constructs and that both can contribute toward the prediction of intention.

Limitations of the Model. The Triandis model has a number of limitations. In contrast to the Fishbein and Ajzen model, the measurement procedures for assessing the various constructs in the model are not delineated clearly; these procedures also have not been evaluated in terms of their psychometric properties (i.e., their reliability and validity). For example, the specific measures to assess facilitating conditions have not been established and have led different researchers to use different measures to assess this construct. One consequence of these diverse measurement procedures is that differences across studies can be attributed to procedural differences and not to substantive or conceptual interpretations. The measurement of affect and self-concept is equally untested. In contrast, the components of the Fishbein and Ajzen model (i.e., intention, attitude, and subjective norm) have received rigorous psychometric testing.

A second limitation of this model is that the components that comprise the social determinants construct are likely to be multidimensional. Thus, the development of a single index to represent social pressure would be unwarranted. Little evidence has been presented to demonstrate that norms, roles, self-concept, and moral norm should be combined to form a single construct. Moreover, there is no evidence to indicate that the integration rule for combining these constructs should be additive. If researchers continue to use this model as a predictor of intention and behavior, then the measurement of the components in the model should be evaluated in terms of their reliability and construct, convergent, and discriminant validity prior to extensive applications of this model.

A third limitation of the model focuses on the uncertainty of where the evaluation of facilitating conditions should occur; that is, should the evaluation of the ease or difficulty of the behavior be determined by an "objective" judge or by the individual? Data are needed to assess this issue. A fourth limitation of this model is the measurement of habit. Triandis measures this construct as the frequency with which the behavior has been performed in the past. This approach allows the measurement of past behavior to be unbounded; that is, past behavior may have occurred in the past with such high frequency that a simple frequency measure may be meaningless (e.g., the number of times an individual has eaten a cookie in the past). Research needs to resolve the issue concerning the appropriate scale on which to measure past behavior. For example, past behavior may be related to future behavior in a nonmonotonic relationship (such as a negatively accelerated curve), and the measurement of habit should allow for an accurate assessment of the relationship between past and future behavior. Finally, all of the limitations described for the intention component of the Fishbein and Ajzen model also are applicable to the Triandis model (e.g., use of regression weights, scaling of beliefs, salience, nomothetic analysis).

Application of the Triandis Model. Few researchers have applied the Triandis model to the study of food-related behavior. Brinberg and Durand (1983) examined the accuracy of the behavioral component of the Triandis model for predicting an individual's behavior of "eating at a fast-food restaurant in the next two weeks." These authors found that intention was significantly correlated with behavior ($r = 0.41$) and that neither habit nor facilitating conditions contributed to the prediction of behavior beyond the contribution of intention. Feldman and Mayhew (1984) applied both the behavioral and intention aspects of the Triandis model in predicting sodium and meat consumption. Both habit and intention contributed significantly in the prediction of these two behaviors ($r = 0.83$ and 0.80, respectively). Facilitating conditions contributed significantly to the prediction of sodium consumption, but not to meat consumption. Feldman and Mayhew (1984) combined these three variables (i.e., habit, intention, and behavior) in an additive manner rather than the multiplicative model proposed by Triandis; therefore, an accurate evaluation of the behavioral component of the Triandis model cannot be determined from their data. The intention component of the model included affect, consequences, norms, and moral norms, and this model was found to be significantly related to the intention to consume meat and sodium (r = 0.63 and 0.61, respectively). The constructs of roles and self-concept were not included in the test of the intention model.

The findings of these two studies indicate that there is conflicting support for the use of constructs other than intention for the prediction of behavior. Brinberg and Durand (1983) found no support for these additional constructs, whereas Feldman and Mayhem (1984) did. Clearly, this area needs research exploring the relations among intention, habit, facilitating conditions, and behavior across a range of food-related behaviors and across a range of respondents to determine the conditions under which these constructs do and do not contribute to the prediction of behavior. If future research is conducted using this model, comparative tests of its effectiveness should be conducted.

Subjective Probability Model

The third model that has been applied to food-related behavior is described as a subjective probability model. As with the Fishbein and Ajzen and Triandis models, the subjective probability model has been tested using a nomothetic (aggregate level) strategy. This probability model was proposed to examine the relationship between beliefs and intention and is expressed as follows (Jaccard and King, 1977):

$$\text{Behavior} \simeq P_i = P_b * P_{i|b} + P_{\bar{b}} * P_{i|\bar{b}}. \tag{6-6}$$

P_i represents an individual's intention to perform the behavior. The relationship between P_i and behavior is hypothesized to be the same as proposed by the Fishbein and Ajzen model; that is, intention is hypothesized to be the best predictor of behavior, and factors such as habit and new information may affect the intention-behavior relationship. P_b represents an individual's perceived probability that performing a certain behavior leads to a particular outcome. This construct is the same as the belief component in the Fishbein and Ajzen and Triandis models, although P_b is measured on a unipolar scale, ranging from 0 to 1, rather than a bipolar scaling ranging from +3 to -3. $P_{i|b}$ represents an individual's perceived probability of intending to perform the behavior, given that the belief is true. This construct is measured by using the following type of question: Suppose that eating at a fast-food hamburger restaurant means getting food that is tasty. How likely are you to eat at this type of restaurant? The respondent is asked to answer this question by using an 11-point, likely/unlikely scale. Typically, this scale is converted to a scale ranging from 0 to 1, with scale values in 0.10 increments. $P_{\bar{b}}$ is the perceived probability that the belief is not true. Typically, this construct is determined by simply subtracting P_b from 1 and is not assessed by asking the respondent the perceived probability of the belief being false. This strategy of determining $P_{\bar{b}}$ assumes that the perceived truth and falsity of a belief is symmetric; that is, the perceived probability of a belief being true and false sum to one. $P_{i|\bar{b}}$ represents an individual's perceived probability of intending to perform the behavior, given the belief is false. This construct is measured by using the following type of question: Suppose that eating at a fast-food hamburger restaurant means getting food that is not tasty. How likely are you to eat at this type of restaurant? The respondent is asked to answer this question by using an 11-point, likely/unlikely scale.

In addition to the prediction of intention, this model is used to identify those beliefs that are important (relevant) to the individual's intention. This model provides a specific index for the importance (relevance) of the belief by using the following equation:

$$|P_{i|b} - P_{i|\bar{b}}|. \tag{6-7}$$

The larger the value, the more relevant that belief is in determining the individual's intention. For instance, suppose that an individual intends to eat at a fast-food restaurant given that the food is tasty (e.g., $P_{i|b} = 0.7$). Further suppose that this individual still intends to eat at a fast-food restaurant given that the food is <u>not</u> tasty (e.g., $P_{i|\overline{b}} = 0.7$). This belief would be irrelevant in determining (and influencing) the individual's intention because that person is likely to eat at a fast-food restaurant whether or not the food is tasty; that is, the relevance index is zero. Now suppose that another individual intends to eat at a fast-food restaurant given that the food is tasty (e.g., $P_{i|b} = 0.7$), but does not intend to eat at a fast-food restaurant given that the food is <u>not</u> tasty (e.g., $P_{i|\overline{b}} = 0.1$). The relevance index would be 0.6, suggesting that this belief is relevant in determining the individual's intention.

When using this model, there is no cutoff point for determining whether a belief should be treated as relevant or irrelevant. The strategy typically used is to rank order the relevance scores and to target beliefs with the highest scores (i.e., the top 2-3 scores) in an education program. To date, only one study (Brinberg and Durand, 1983) has applied the subjective probability model to the study of a food-related behavior--eating at a fast-food restaurant. These researchers found the model to be a significant predictor of intention for each belief (median r between beliefs and intention was 0.52). The key relevant beliefs were taste, quality, and expense (relevance score of 0.63, 0.47, and 0.46, respectively). These authors concluded that the development of advertising (or education programs) should focus on taste, quality and expense because these beliefs are most likely to affect an individual's intention to eat at a fast-food restaurant.

A third feature of the subjective probability model is its ability to predict the amount of change in intention given a change in belief by using the following equation:

$$\Delta P_i = \Delta P_b * |P_{i|b} - P_{i|\overline{b}}|, \qquad (6\text{-}8)$$

where ΔP_i is the amount of change in intention, and ΔP_b is the amount of change in the belief. This equation implies that no change is predicted in intention if either the belief is unchanged or the belief is irrelevant; that is, if either ΔP_b or $|P_{i\,|b} - P_{i\,|\overline{b}}|$ is zero. Clearly, changing intention, according to this model, will occur only when the researcher is able to change a relevant belief. One assumption when using this equation to predict the amount of change in intention is that neither of the two conditional probabilities (i.e., $P_{i\,|b} - P_{i\,|\overline{b}}$) change when the belief is changed.

The beliefs used to test the model are determined by using the same elicitation procedure as described for both the Fishbein and Ajzen and Triandis models. When this model is used to predict intention, the researcher assesses the constructs of the model for each belief. The effectiveness of the model is evaluated in terms of the degree of fit between the intention predicted by the model, for each belief, and the individual's stated intention. The degree of fit is assessed by both the correlation and the absolute deviation between the predicted and stated intention.

Comparison of the Subjective Probability with the Fishbein and Ajzen Model. The Triandis model has not been included because the differences between it and the subjective probability model are comparable to the differences between the Fishbein and Ajzen and the subjective probability model. Both the Fishbein and Ajzen and the subjective probability model use intention to predict behavior, although both models recognize that other factors (e.g., habit) may influence the intention-behavior relationship. These two models differ, however, in their prediction of intention. In the Fishbein and Ajzen model, a distinction is made between attitudinal and normative beliefs, whereas in the subjective probability model, no distinction is made between these beliefs. That is, both attitudinal and normative beliefs may be included in the model as beliefs, but not as a "certain type of belief." In addition, several other constructs are included in the Fishbein and Ajzen model that are not used in the subjective probability model; that is, an overall measure of evaluation and social pressure. The subjective probability model only uses measures of beliefs.

Although related to intention differently, the concept of belief is included in both models. In the subjective probability model, the relationship between a belief and intention is described by the laws of objective probability. Research using this model has related each belief to intention. The Fishbein and Ajzen model uses an expectancy-value formulation and includes the sum of the "salient" beliefs and their evaluations to predict attitude (or consequences). An important implication of both of these integration rules (i.e., separate analysis of each belief and the summation of the salient beliefs) is that the beliefs do not interact with each other; that is, values on one belief do not affect the values on other beliefs. Both models would assume, for example, that perceptions of quality would be unrelated to perceptions of price. Both social judgment theory and the behavioral alternatives model (to be presented) allow for an assessment of this assumption.

Fishbein and Ajzen (1975) argue that the salient beliefs determine an individual's attitude and subjective norm. Salience is a construct used to identify psychologically important beliefs. As noted previously, these beliefs are identified through an open-ended elicitation process. According to this theory, modifying the salient beliefs will change individuals' attitudes (or subjective norm) and, thus, their intention. The limitations associated with the construct of salience were presented in the discussion of the Fishbein and Ajzen model. In the subjective probability model, the difference between the two conditional probabilities is used to quantify the degree to which a belief will influence an individual's intention.

A final difference between these models is that the Fishbein and Ajzen model uses regression coefficients to measure the relative importance of the various constructs in each model. The subjective probability model, on the other hand, uses the relevance score as an index of importance rather than regression coefficients.

Limitations of the Model. One limitation of the subjective probability model is that only the logical (probabilistic) relationships among beliefs and intention are assumed to be needed to understand the determinants of intention. Several researchers (e.g., Fishbein and Ajzen, 1975; Triandis, 1977) provide evidence to suggest that this assumption is not cogent. For example, attitude (which is not included in the subjective probability model) is consistently a significant determinant of intention (see Table 6-1). A second limitation is the assumption that the beliefs are independent and can be analyzed separately when examining intention. Current research (e.g., Jaccard and Wood, 1986) suggests that the assumption of independence may be violated and that the perceived value of one belief may affect the perceived value of another (such as the perceived relationship between price and quality).

Social Judgment Theory

This theory has its roots in the work of Egon Brunswik (1955) and has provided the foundation for a significant body of research in the area of judgment and decision making. Although this theory has not been applied to the study of food-related behavior, it is clearly a framework that could be used to provide some insights into people's decisions related to food selection.

Two basic principles underlie Brunswikian designs: the use of representative rather than systematic experiments and the use of idiographic rather than nomothetic analysis. Systematic designs are typified by the ANOVA (analysis of variance) factorial design in which a small number of variables are treated as independent (i.e., orthogonal) to each other. In other words, the researcher disentangles the actual interrelations among the variables and treats them as if they are independent of each other. For example, a researcher may be interested in examining the effect of situational variables on eating away from home. She could create a systematic design by using two variables manipulated on two levels (e.g., one factor could be the convenience of going to the restaurant, with two levels, close or far, and the other factor cost of the restaurant, with two levels, high or low). Individuals who participate in this 2 x 2 factorial-design experiment are asked to rate the likelihood of their going to the restaurant given the particular combination of attributes (e.g., a close restaurant that is inexpensive). Representative designs, on the other hand, allow for the natural variations among the variables and do not attempt to separate the interrelationships among the variables. Using the previous example, individuals would be asked to rate a variety of restaurants that differ in convenience and cost in terms of the likelihood of their going to each restaurant.

The second basic principle underlying social judgment theory is the use of an idiographic perspective. This perspective is described by contrasting systematic and representative designs. In the systematic design, individuals are sampled and treated as replicates in the design; that is, the error term (and the degrees of freedom) are affected (and determined) by the number of individuals who participate in the study. In effect, the researcher attempts to generalize across individuals (by having multiple individuals in the study), but only uses a single representation of the situation. In the representative design, situations are sampled and treated as replicates in the design; that is, the error term (and the degrees of freedom) are affected (and determined) by the number of situations used in the study and not the number of subjects. In effect, the researcher attempts to generalize across situations for each individual. Individual results then can be aggregated to determine the patterns that exist across respondents; that is, clusters of individuals can be formed to represent homogeneous responses to the various situations.

Social judgment theory is characterized by the Brunswik Lens Model. This model is used to examine the relationship between cues (e.g., food attributes) and 1) an environmental (external) criterion (e.g., whether a nutrition educator views the food as good for you/bad for you), and 2) the individual's judgment (e.g., whether the individual views the food as good for you/bad for you). Figure 6-1 portrays the Brunswik Lens model.

In this model, $r_{e,i}$ represents the correlation of each cue (attribute) with the nutrition educator's judgment (external criterion), and $r_{s,i}$ represents the correlation between each cue and the individual's judgment. For example, suppose that a researcher is interested in examining an individual's perception of whether foods are good for you/bad for you and comparing this individual's perceptions to the perceptions of a nutrition educator. Furthermore, suppose that the individual is given the following information about the food: x_1 = the food's fiber content; x_2 = the food's sodium content; x_3 = the food's fat content; and x_4 = the food's protein content.

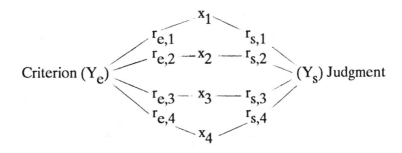

Fig. 6-1. The Brunswik lens model

When using this model, the researcher would create a variety of foods that vary on these four cues, and both the expert and the individual would be asked to judge whether the food is good for you/bad for you. Suppose that each cue had four values (e.g., fiber values were 1 g, 3 g, 5 g, and 7 g). Both the expert and the individual would be asked to make 256 judgments (i.e., unique combinations of the 4 x 4 x 4 x 4 cues). The quantitative analysis of the lens model is conducted by using the following equation:

$$r_a = GR_1R_2 + C \sqrt{(1 - R_1^2) * (1 - R_2^2)}, \qquad (6\text{-}9)$$

where r_a is the correlation between the individual's and the expert's judgment. G is the correlation between the predicted scores derived from the two models, i.e., the model used to predict the expert's rating and the model used to predict the individual's rating. These models are determined by using regression analysis. Another interpretation of G is the individual's knowledge of the foods; that is, G represents the correlation between the individual's and the expert's judgments of the foods. R_1 is a measure of fit between the cues and the expert's judgment, and R_2 is a measure of fit between the cues and the individual's judgment. C is the extent to which nonlinear variance of one model is related to the nonlinear variance of the other model; that is, C is the correlation between the residuals from the linear regressions of Y_e and Y_s. If the C value is high, then there is a consistent nonlinear variation that is common to the two models.

The lens model has been used to examine a variety of factors that influence judgment. One set of studies has examined the effect of cue characteristics on an individual's judgment; e.g., the effect of the number of cues, the redundancy among the cues, and the metric characteristics of the cues (e.g., ratio, interval, ordinal, and nominal). A second set of studies has examined the relative importance of the cues, the functional relations between the cues and the external criterion, and the integration rule used to combine the cues (e.g., additive versus configural--a model that allows for an interaction among the cues).

Although the lens model has not been applied to food-related behavior, some previous applications of the model may suggest avenues for future research. One area of research has examined learning (this area of research has been called multiple-cue probability learning). These researchers have examined the types of cues to which individuals attend when making a judgment. For example, researchers have examined the difference between what the individual states is important to him or her when making a decision and the actual empirical weights when the lens model is used. Where differences occur between the subjective and empirically-derived weights, individuals are informed of these differences and allowed to either revise their own subjective weight or "learn" to weight the cues in a way to give the appropriate (empirical) weight to a cue. For example, suppose that an individual states that he uses the amount of fiber in food as an important determinant in his judgment of whether a food is beneficial to health. Further suppose that the empirical weight $r_{s,1}$ is very low. The difference between these two weights would be presented to the individual to indicate that his judgment is not affected by the cue, even though the individual states that the cue is important. If the individual chooses not to reassess the subjective weight, he or she can be instructed to place greater weight on that cue.

The comparison of the social judgment model with the other models is combined with the discussion of the behavioral alternatives model (to be presented in the next section) because many of the issues associated with the two models are the similar.

Limitations of the Model. One limitation of the social judgment theory is that no criteria for selecting the cues for the study are given. In contrast, the nomothetic models do provide some guidance by suggesting the technique of open-ended elicitations for selecting salient beliefs. A second limitation is the number of stimuli needed to develop a stable estimate of the decision rules used by an individual. Because the linear model is very robust, nonlinear components may not be detected, even though they do affect an individual's decision.

Behavioral Alternatives Model

Jaccard (Jaccard and Wood, 1986) has developed a theory of decision making (described as a behavioral alternatives model) that can be used to assess the determinants of an individual's decision. This theory states that an individual will select an alternative from among a set of alternatives toward which the most positive attitude is held. The methodology developed to test this model allows the researcher to examine: 1) the individual's preferences and decision rules used to select from among a set of alternatives (e.g., foods), and

2) the relationships among the types of alternatives (e.g., foods) and attributes considered to be important (e.g., cost, taste, healthfulness) when selecting an alternative.

Specifically, the behavioral alternatives model is an attitude-based model for predicting and understanding choice behavior. The model is concerned with the situation where an individual can perform one of **n** alternative behaviors (e.g., to select from one of **n** foods) and is concerned with identifying which factors will influence an individual's choice. Using food choice as the frame for describing this theory, the individual is said to possess an attitude toward selecting a number of different foods, where the attitude is the evaluation of the food on a bipolar scale (e.g., favorable/unfavorable). For a selection among a set of **n** foods, there are **n** attitudes, one toward each food. The set of attitudes is called a preference structure. The behavioral alternatives model would predict that an individual will decide to select that alternative toward which the most positive attitude is held.

Once the individual's preference structure (i.e., his or her's overall evaluation of each option) is determined, the researcher then assesses the person's evaluation of each option on a set of attributes. This set of option-attribute ratings is described as a perceptual structure.

Both the perceptual and preference structures provide substantial detail concerning the individual's decision process. For example, suppose that a nutrition educator is interesting in increasing the consumption of beans (because of its dietary fiber content) from among a set of food options (e.g., corn, peas, and spinach). The evaluation of each food option (i.e., the preference structure) is measured by having the respondent evaluate each food on a good/bad scale. Suppose that an individual had a positive evaluation of beans and corn and a negative evaluation of peas and spinach. Two basic strategies can be used to increase the consumption of beans. One strategy would be to increase (make more positive) the individual's attitude toward the beans. The second strategy would be to decrease (make more negative) the individual's attitude toward peas. The specific factors (attributes) on which to focus are determined by an analysis of the perceptual structure. Jaccard (Jaccard and Wood, 1986) notes that the greater the difference between the choices (i.e., the food options), the more stable the behavior will be over time and the more likely the person will be to select the option toward which he or she holds the most positive evaluation.

Now suppose that the same individual is asked to rate these foods on a set of attributes. For instance, an individual may be asked to rate corn on the attributes of taste, cost, and healthfulness by using an 11-point, good/bad scale and peas in terms of the same attributes and so on. Based on the data matrix generated for this individual, several types of analyses can be conducted.

One set of analyses examines the perceived similarity among the foods. Given **p** foods and **m** attributes, a **p** x **p** symmetric similarity matrix can be calculated. The dissimilarity between any two foods, i and j, is defined as follows:

$$d_{ij} = 1/m \; \Sigma \; (R_{ki} - R_{kj})^2 \tag{6-10}$$

where d_{ij} is the dissimilarity between foods i and j, R_{ki} is the rating of food i on attribute k, and R_{kj} is the rating of food j on attribute k. This cluster analysis can be used to identify, for a given food, which other foods are perceived as similar. This information could be useful when developing a nutrition education program. Respondents could be encouraged to eat foods that are perceived as similar, but which differ along a particular dimension (such as fiber content); that is, foods perceived as similar may be viewed by the individual as substitutable.

A second cluster analysis can be used to examine the relations among the attributes. This type of analysis would yield information concerning the perceived similarity among different attributes; for example, convenience and price may be viewed within the same cluster. Given **m** attributes, an **m** x **m** symmetric matrix will result.

The dissimilarity between any two attributes i and j is defined as follows:

$$d_{ij} = 1/p \Sigma (R_{iq} - R_{jq})^2, \qquad (6\text{-}11)$$

where d_{ij} is the dissimilarity between attributes i and j, R_{iq} is the rating of attribute i on food q, and R_{jq} is the rating of attribute j on food q. This cluster analysis can be used to provide insights concerning the perceived similarity among attributes and would indicate which attributes would be substitutable in an education program. For instance, suppose that the educator finds price and convenience to be perceived as similar. In developing the education program, either of these attributes can be used in the message.

The behavioral alternatives model also allows the researcher to determine the decision rule that the individual uses to select which foods to eat. This model adopts an information integration paradigm (Anderson, 1981) to examine the trade-offs an individual uses when he or she combines information to reach a decision. A detailed discussion of this procedure may be found in Anderson (1981) and Jaccard and Wood (1986). But, briefly, this approach assumes that the decision process is composed of three separate processes: valuation, integration, and response subprocesses. Valuation is the process by which the individual assigns meaning to a particular stimulus; e.g., gives meaning to the attribute of "convenient to obtain." Integration is the process by which the individual combines the separate stimuli into a unified response. Response is the process by which the individual makes the internal integration overt by responding on some type of scale; e.g., evaluating the stimulus on a particular rating scale.

In a typical information integration experiment, the researcher presents information (e.g., food attributes) to the individual and asks the individual to make a judgment (e.g., to evaluate a food that has a particular combination of attributes). For example, suppose that the individual was presented with information concerning three food attributes---cost, healthfulness, and preparation.

Further suppose that each of the attributes is presented in terms of three levels--low, medium, and high cost; bad, neutral, and good in terms of healthfulness; and difficult, neutral, and easy in terms of preparation. These three food attributes and three levels results in a 3 x 3 x 3 factorial design. The individual is asked to evaluate a "hypothetical" food that has characteristics described by combinations of the three attributes; for example, the individual is asked to evaluate a food that is low in cost, good on healthfulness, and easy to prepare on a 7-point, good/bad scale. The respondent rates each of the 27 "hypothetical" foods. Based on these judgments, the integration rules used to combine the information can be derived. Analysis of variance procedures are used to analyze the responses in this 3 x 3 x 3 factorial design. For example, if the attributes are combined in an additive manner (i.e., consistent with an expectancy-value model), there will be no interaction among the three factors in the design. If an interaction does exist, however, this finding suggests a nonadditive model, and the nature of the interaction can be determined by post-hoc analysis. For example, some research (e.g., Lynch, 1979) has found that a differential weighted averaging model describes the integration rule for combining information, where negative information receives a greater weight than positive information (i.e., it has a greater impact of the individual's judgment), and the information is averaged rather than added.

Comparison of the Five Models. There are a number of differences between the idiographic (behavioral alternatives model and social judgment theory) and the nomothetic models (Fishbein and Ajzen, Triandis, and subjective probability model). One major difference between these two types of models is the unit of analysis; that is, a within-subject versus a between-subject perspective. As noted before, the major limitation of the nomothetic (between-subject) models is the inability of these models to provide information on the decision process of an individual. A second major difference between these two types of models is the constructs included in the models. The behavioral alternatives model views the choice process as a selection from among a set of alternatives, and the most likely choice is that behavior toward which the individual has the most positive attitude. Social judgment theory views the decision process as a function of cues (i.e., attributes/beliefs). Each of the three nomothetic models uses constructs other than attitude and cues (beliefs) to predict behavior. For example, Triandis (1977) uses habit and facilitating conditions in addition to intention to predict behavior. Fishbein and Ajzen (1975) use intention as the primary predictor of behavior. Third, the nomothetic models impose an additive integration, whereas the behavioral alternatives model and social judgment theory can diagnose the decision rule used by the individual.

Similarities exist among the models. First, each model uses beliefs, but combines them in different ways. Second, the Fishbein and Ajzen, Triandis, and behavioral alternatives model use the concept of attitude as a determinant of intention (or behavior).

Limitations of the Model. Because the behavioral alternatives model has received few empirical tests, no research exists that discusses the limitations of the model. On a pragmatic level, however, there are several limitations. To obtain meaningful, stable clusters of options (e.g., foods) and attributes (e.g., food characteristics), a sufficient number of options and attributes needs to be rated. The substantial number of ratings makes the judgment tasks lengthy and somewhat difficult to administer. A second limitation is the assumption that the items treated as replicates (attributes when the cluster analysis is of options and options when the cluster analysis is of attributes) are independent and equally weighted. If an option or attribute is substantially different than the other options or attributes in the set, then the solutions from the cluster analyses may be affected adversely.

Application of the Behavioral Alternatives Model. To date, there are no direct applications of the behavioral alternatives model toward the analysis of food-related behavior. Michela and Contento (1986) and Contento, Michela, and Goldberg (1988), however, have applied a perspective quite similar to the behavioral alternatives model. These authors examined food choices among children and adolescents and used an idiographic perspective to identify subgroups in the population. Although their focus was on a segmentation strategy, these authors first determined the relationship among the food options and food attributes for each individual prior to creating the subgroups. In addition to this segmentation of the sample, their data also can be analyzed to create food groupings for each individual in order to create nutrition education messages designed for the specific food preferences and perceptions of that individual.

7

"Without concepts, mental life would be chaotic. If we perceived each entity as unique, we would be overwhelmed by the sheer diversity of what we experience and unable to remember more than a minute fraction of what we encounter. And if each individual entity needed a distinct name, our language would be staggeringly complex and communication virtually impossible." (Smith and Medin, 1981, pg 1)

According to Smith and Medin (1981), concepts (and classes) are essential for understanding and communicating our experiences. Likewise, in food and nutrition, concepts and classes not only allow communication among professionals in the field, but also allow communication between professionals and the public. In fact, food and nutrition educators have considered one type of classification system, food guides, an indispensable tool for communicating to the public the information needed to obtain adequate amounts of nutrients. These food guides reflect a distillation of a large and complex body of knowledge about human nutrition and foods into a few potentially understandable concepts that can be used by the consumer. Considering how central these systems are to the field, it is rather surprising to discover that there seems to be more discussion about the ability of these systems to communicate the desired information rather than any research to determine their effectiveness as understandable food guidance systems.

Because the use of classification systems by professionals to communicate with the public is so common, it is essential to understand exactly what a classification system is in order to evaluate the issues embedded in the ongoing discussion of the appropriateness of various food guides. This chapter is divided into three parts. First, definitions of classification systems are discussed. This part is followed by a presentation of professionals' food classification systems and the properties on which they are based. Third, research concerning food grouping systems from the consumers' perspective will be addressed.

Definitions

Class is defined as "a group, set, or kind sharing common attributes," according to Webster's *New Collegiate Dictionary* (1979). In other words, when objects are grouped together because they are considered to have similar characteristics, these objects form a class. Fruits would be an example of a class. Most people would classify apples, oranges, and strawberries as fruits because these items share common attributes (characteristics), perhaps like sweet tasting, used for dessert, are composed of the soft, pulpy portion surrounding the seeds of a plant after it flowers, and so forth.

A term related to class is concept, which Webster (1979) defines as "an abstract or generic idea generalized from particular instances." An example of a commonly used concept in food and nutrition is good health. Good health is an abstract idea that is derived by examining some particular instances. Saying that a person is considered to be in good health could mean that person is free of disease, experiences no pain, has a cholesterol level below 200 mg/dl, has a Body Mass Index between 18-25, and so forth. Going back to the previous example, fruit also could be considered a concept because it is an abstract idea which is derived from particular cases-- e.g., apples, oranges, and strawberries.

These two definitions, taken together, delineate three essential aspects of classification systems (Note: the terms concept and class will be used interchangeably.) First, a class is an abstraction. Fruit and good health, for example, are simply abstractions--in reality, neither exists as a particular instance or case. Second, a class is composed of a group of specific objects, instances, or cases. Third, the objects, instances, and cases in a class are perceived to have common properties or attributes. In other words, one idea or one word is an abstract representation of a number of specific cases or instances which have some properties or attributes in common. Concepts and classes are considered stable within a person over time and considered fairly stable across people, i.e., most people use the concepts and classes in a similar manner.

An attribute is an inherent characteristic of an object, which contributes to but does not provide a complete description of the object; consequently, there usually will be more than one attribute to represent a class. An attribute can be called a dimension or a feature, depending on the nature of the attribute. An attribute is called a dimension when it represents an underlying continuum like sweetness, whereby the sweetness of an object can range from very sweet to not at all sweet. On the other hand, an attribute is called a feature when it represents a category, that is, the object either possesses it or not. For example, a feature of a person is his or her gender (i.e., male or female). A dimension of a person could be his or her perceived masculinity/femininity. Smith and Medin (1981) state that when objects are described by using dimensions, only a small number of dimensions are needed and every object will have some value on each dimension. In contrast, when objects are described by using features, it is likely that many features will be needed and that some features will apply to some objects in the class but not others. For example, if the class to be described was food, one feature like "plant product" would apply to some objects in the class but not others. Thus, this feature would apply to apples but not fish.

Cognitive psychologists spend a lot of their time studying how people acquire, use, and structure concepts and classes. In this section, only the structure of classes will be discussed because the acquisition and use of classification systems related to food and nutrition have not been studied to any extent. The following discussion relies on Smith and Medin's (1981) explanation of the issues surrounding the conceptualization of categories and concepts.

There are three views concerning the structure of concepts: the classical, the probabilistic, and the exemplar. Smith and Medin (1981, pg 3) explain that the three schools of thought can be best described by the way in which they would answer the following questions (Table 7.1): 1) Is there a single or unitary description for all members of the class? And, 2) are the properties specified in a unitary description true of all members of the class?

Table 7.1

Answers to Two Critical Questions About Class Structure According to the Classical, Probabilistic, and Exemplar Views

Viewpoint	**Question 1** Unitary description for all class members?	**Question 2** Description applicable to all class members?
Classical	Yes	Yes
Probabilistic	Yes	No
Exemplar	No	Not applicable

The *classical view* holds that a class can be represented by a single description, and this description is comprised of the necessary and sufficient attributes (properties) which represent the class of objects, instances, or cases. Necessary and sufficient means that all of the attributes in the description must be present (necessary) and that no other attributes besides the ones in the description are needed (sufficient). Second, the classical view holds that these attributes used in the summary description will apply to all members of the class. According to Smith and Medin (1981), the classical view is concerned with summary descriptions that use only features. In addition, this view is interested primarily in those features which reveal relations among concepts and classes and not necessarily features which people use to categorize objects. To illustrate these points, let's take casserole as an example of a class. First, a summary description could include four features (attributes): the object is a food mixture (1st feature) which is baked (2d feature) and served (3rd feature) in a deep dish (4th feature). According to the classical view, any object with these features would be classified as a casserole. Thus, the four features would be singly necessary (all would have to be present) and jointly sufficient (no others are needed) to characterize this concept-- a casserole.   Macaroni and cheese, because it possesses all four attributes (it is a food mixture which is baked and served in a deep dish), would be classified as a casserole. Another food that would fit into the casserole class, based on this summary description, would be a deep-pan pizza--it is a food mixture, baked and served in a deep dish. Most people, however, would not classify pizza as a casserole. Possible resolutions to this problem are discussed after examining the probabilistic view.

The *probabilistic view* is similar to the classical view in that a class can be represented by a single description, but differs from the classical view in that the attributes specified in the description are not necessary and sufficient. In other words, the probabilistic view holds that a summary description of a class is possible and that this description is comprised of attributes which the members of the class possess. These attributes outlined in the summary description, however, do not necessarily apply to all members in the class. According to the probabilistic view, the attributes used in the summary description are not restricted to a set of necessary and sufficient attributes. Rather, the probabilistic view holds that the attributes used to represent a class are most likely the prominent ones which most, but not necessarily all, class members possess. In other words, the attributes are "some sort of measure of central tendency of the objects' properties or patterns," according to Smith and Medin (1981). Thus, the classical view holds that the features used in the summary description are necessary and sufficient, whereas the probabilistic view holds that the attributes used in the summary description are the prominent ones which have a substantial probability of occurring. Investigators within the probabilistic school have developed models to describe the structure of classes by using both dimensions and features. In addition, these investigators are interested in those attributes which people use to categorize objects as well as those attributes which would illuminate the relationships among concepts (Smith and Medin, 1981).

To illustrate the difference between the classical and probabilistic views, let's return to the casserole and ask this question--would a macaroni and cheese dish which had been cooked on the top of the stove instead of baked in the oven be classified as a casserole? From the probabilistic view, this stove-top macaroni and cheese dish could be classified as a casserole because the features used in the summary description are not considered necessary and sufficient but only probable. Thus, even though one feature in the particular instance does not match the features in the summary description, if people classify this object as a casserole, it would not be considered an error in classification by the probabilistic view. The probabilistic view would argue that people classify objects by matching the features of a particular instance to the features of the summary description of class. If these featural "matches" hit a critical point, then the object is categorized into the class, or if a "match" was not made, it was because the critical point was not reached. From the classical view, this stove-top macaroni and cheese dish should not be classified as a casserole because it does not contain the necessary and sufficient features, i.e., baked and served in a deep dish.

The deep-pan pizza provides another example by which to examine the differences in the two views. This time the particular instance possesses all of the features contained in the summary description, and most people should classify deep-pan pizza as a casserole; however, most people would not. The classical view would view this as a classification error and would probably give one of several explanations for this error: 1) people may have an incomplete or poor grasp of the concept so that they make errors in categorizing some objects, 2) there can be two types of summary definitions--one technical and one common, and in this case the common summary description may not match the technical one, and 3) the summary description may be wrong, i.e., the necessary and sufficient features have not been delineated. An investigator holding a probabilistic view might explain this error by saying that there is a low probability that any summary description will allow a perfect classification of objects. Rather, a good summary description will allow a significant number of objects to be categorized correctly.

The *exemplar view* is different from both the classical and probabilistic views. First, the exemplar view holds that classes are represented by their exemplars (ideal models or examples) rather than by an abstract summary description. Thus, the exemplar view differs from the other views in the level of abstraction of class description. The representation of a class from the exemplar view is less abstract in that the exemplar (representation) can either be a specific instance or a specific subset of that class. Second, the exemplar view does not address the issue of general attributes or properties of a class because it does not hold that there are summary descriptions. Rather, a class is seen as being represented by a number of exemplars, and each exemplar has its own description (or set of properties). Hence, the classical and probabilistic views hold that there are abstract representations of classes, and the objects in a class share common properties, whereas the exemplar view holds that specific objects (or relevant subsets of objects) are the representation of a class, and that there is no summary description of the class, only descriptions related to different exemplars. Let's return again to the example of the casserole. From the exemplar viewpoint, the concept of casserole could be represented by a number of exemplars. When an object like the stove-top macaroni and cheese is presented to someone for classi-fication, the exemplar view holds that the person would probably retrieve an example and examine both the example and the object to see whether they match. In this case, the person might retrieve a baked macaroni and cheese as the exemplar and decide that the stove-top macaroni and cheese was a match. When presented with the deep-pan pizza, the person might retrieve the exemplar of macaroni and cheese and decide it was not a match, or the person might even retrieve an exemplar from another concept which matches better and thus decide it is not a casserole but an Italian dish.

The primary function of classes is that they provide an orderly system by which to view the world; meaning, when presented with a specific object, a person uses his or her classification system as a struc-ture by which an object can be categorized. Let's say that a new food product comes on the market. This new product has the following attributes--crunchy, salty, formed like a wafer, and comes in a cello-phane package. Investigators using the classical view probably would not be interested in this problem because 1) some of the attributes are dimensions (e.g., salty) and 2) this problem focuses on the attributes which people use to categorize an object. The probabilistic school, however, would be interested in this problem and would predict that the consumer would examine the attributes of this new product and categorize it in a class that has similar attributes--such as, it has the same attributes as a snack food; thus, it must be a snack food. The exemplar view would predict that the consumer would say, this product seems to be like a potato chip, and thus place it in the class that contains potato chips. In this case, the crucial claim of the exemplar view is that the exemplar plays the dominant role in catego-rization, whereas the claim of the probabilistic view is that the summary information (i.e., attributes or properties) of the object plays the dominant role in categorization.

Professionals' Food Guides

The primary objective of national food guides has stayed fairly constant over time (see, for example, the reviews of the history of food guides in the U.S. by Hertzler and Anderson, 1974; Light and Cronin, 1981). The historic objective of national food guides (developed primarily by employees of the U.S. Department of Agriculture) has been to translate currently accepted dietary standards into nutrition education tools easily understood and used by people in the general population to select nutritionally adequate diets (Hertzler and Anderson, 1974; Light and Cronin, 1981). When developing these food guides, food and nutrition professionals have relied on classification systems--that is, they have developed abstract representations (e.g., food groups) of a number of specific objects (e.g., foods) which have some properties or attributes in common.

Food guides are considered professionals' food classification systems not because professionals developed the classification systems, but rather because these food guides must meet the criteria embedded in the classes and concepts used by professionals in the food and nutrition field (e.g., the translation of dietary standards into nutrition education tools). Only secondly are the consumers' ability to use the guide considered. One of the most recently published food guides provides a good example of this point. The authors state that

> "this food guidance system provides the more specific information needed to implement the Dietary Guidelines. Within the system, a framework of food groups . . . provides the core around which other nutrition information is organized. This framework groups foods commonly available in the United States by the nutrients they contain, while maintaining categories that are potentially recognized by consumers" (Cronin *et al.*, 1987, pg 282).

Food guides are more than just a classification system. These food guides have two components: 1) the classification system, which is usually some groupings of food, and 2) the guide, which is usually a suggested minimum number of servings which should be consumed by individuals from each food group in the classification system. The first component, the classification system, represents the cognitive component of the food guide. These classification systems provide the cognitive structure which is used by nutritionists to communicate some basic concepts. The second component, the guide, represents the behavior or action component of the food guide. This portion translates the concepts outlined in the cognitive component into discrete behaviors or actions which individuals should undertake to comply with the information given in the classification system.

> "In order to develop food guides that are nutritionally valid and readily understood, USDA traditionally has considered a variety of data sources, including information on the nutritional and dietary status of the population, dietary standards, food consumption practices, food availability, nutritive composition of foods, and food costs." (Light and Cronin, 1981, pg 57)

> "Nutritional and dietary status, food patterns, food availability, nutritive value of foods, and food economics have been considerations in developing nutritionally reliable food guides from the first one of 1916 to the current guide. Simplicity has been attained by limiting the number of food groups in the plans and by using familiar names of foods." (Hertzler and Anderson, 1974, pg 27)

Light and Cronin (1981) and Hertzler and Anderson (1974) in separate reviews come up with similar lists of the criteria used to develop the food guides. To examine the criteria on which the classification systems within these food guides have been based, it is necessary to separate the criteria for the classification component from the criteria for the guidance component of the guide. Of the criteria listed by Light and Cronin (1981) and Hertzler and Anderson (1974), nutritional requirements of the population seemed to be the most instrumental in developing the guidance component of the guides. The other criteria--dietary status of the population, food consumption patterns, food availability, nutritive composition of foods, food costs, familiar names of foods, and simplicity--seemed to have a greater impact on the classification component. The criteria used for the guidance component seem to be goals or standards (e.g., RDAs). These standards provide the basic information which the authors use when making decisions about which behaviors should be promoted in the guidance component. The criteria used for the classification component seem to be descriptions of foods and food-related practices. These descriptions provide the basic information which the authors use when making decisions about which concepts should be incorporated into the classification system. Because the criteria used by the authors are given most often for the entire food guide and not broken down by components, the manner in which the criteria are assigned to components reflects an educated guess regarding the authors' thoughts.

Guidance criteria. The guidance component of a food guide provides the plan of action for individuals, and the two criteria most often used to develop these plans have been nutritional requirements of the population and dietary standards. These plans for action have varied over time with the advent of new or more complete information. For example, Light and Cronin (1981) explain that up until the late 1940s, the food guides stressed the balance in the diet between the nutrient-dense foods and energy-dense foods. As indicated by the publication of the Four Food Groups guide by the USDA in 1957, the emphasis of food guides changed to promoting foundation diets based on the consumption of nutrient-dense foods. This change in emphasis reflected a greater knowledge of nutrient requirements, food composition, and dietary status of the population. These guides translated the Recommended Dietary Allowances (RDAs were first published in the early 1940s) into actions to meet these nutrient allowances. Presently, the food guides based on the philosophy of the 1950s are being re-evaluated because of again new and more complete information about nutrient requirements, food composition, and dietary status of the population. Now, researchers are suggesting that not only the RDAs serve as a standard by which to measure dietary guidance, but also the various dietary guidelines and goals (published by a number of federal agencies and professional organizations), which tend to caution against the overconsumption of various food constituents like sodium, sugar, and fat. Pennington (1981, pg 53) sums up the new objective of food guides very well when she says that "Any new food guide should accommodate alternative food choice behavior within the constraint of ensuring adequate intake of essential nutrients while preventing excesses of energy or other food constituents." An example of one of these newer food guides is The Food Wheel: A Pattern for Daily Food Choices, developed by Cronin and her associates (1987). When developing their food guidance system, they established their nutritional goals based on the 1980 RDAs and the first edition of the Dietary Guidelines.

Most of the evaluation and criticism of food guides has focused on the Four Food Groups guide (USDA, 1957), probably because 1) it is the food guide thought to be best known by consumers and the most widely used in nutrition education, and 2) more recently developed food guides are modifications of the Four Food Groups guide. The most common criticisms are that the Four Food Groups guide does not ensure nutrient adequacy, does not address current dietary problems of the population, and is an ineffective communication tool (Light and Cronin, 1981). The first two criticisms relate to dietary adequacy and dietary problems and have direct implications for the guidance component of the guide; the ability of the guide to be an effective communication tool has implications for both components of the guide.

One example of these criticisms is the work done by King and co-workers (1978). They questioned whether the Four Food Groups guide still provided useful dietary guidance because the RDAs on which the guide had been based had been changed a number of times (i.e., nutrient allowances changed or added). They (1978) evaluated the Four Food Groups guide by 1) calculating the average nutrient content of 20 full-day menus published as examples of good diets based on the food guide and 2) comparing the nutrient content of these menus against the 1974 RDAs. The results of the menu analysis indicated that on average half of the nutrients evaluated in the study did not meet the recommended allowances. Based on this finding, they proposed a Modified Basic Four, which essentially outlines a much more specific plan of action. Even though they call it their Modified Basic Four, King *et al.* (1978) included a fat and oil group (with a suggested number of servings), subdivided the protein group into animal protein and legumes and/or nuts (with suggested servings), and subdivided the fruits and vegetables groups into vitamin C-rich, dark green, and other (again with suggested servings). In addition, they proposed a Modified Basic Four guide for special preferences: no meat, no milk, no legumes, and low cost.

As mentioned before, the Four Food Groups guide also has been criticized for not being an effective communication tool; specifically, the presentation of the food groups (cognitive structure) does not reflect the guidance component (behavior recommendations) of the food guide. For example, Lachance (1981) suggested that the Four Food Groups should be represented visually to emphasize consumption of foods in the fruit-vegetable group and bread-cereals group. Along this line, Pennington (1981) suggested that the food groups should be represented graphically by an inverted pyramid, which would emphasis recommended levels of consumption (liberal to sparse).

Classification criteria. Whereas professionals have spent a lot of effort establishing the criteria (i.e., the nutritional requirements of the population and dietary standards) for the guidance component of food guides, they have spent little effort establishing the criteria by which to develop and evaluate the classification component. Remembering that a class is an abstract representation of a number of objects which have some properties or attributes in common, the critical questions that must be answered when developing the classification system would include: What type of classes should be used? What common attributes or properties should characterize the groups?

Only two types of classes have been considered as the basis for the classification systems--foods or food constituents. Foods from the beginning have been the preferred type of class. Since the early 1900s, according to Hertzler and Anderson (1974), almost all of the national food guides have had classification systems based on foods rather than food constituents. The creators of these classification systems seem to have felt intuitively that foods provided a common ground on which people in the general population and professionals in the field of food and nutrition could meet. Food constituents, on the other hand, are concepts embedded in the conceptual structure of the food and nutrition field and not readily understood by those outside the field.

Given that foods constitute the type of class, professionals then must decide which attributes or properties should be used to characterize the groups--in other words, on what basis will the foods be assigned to the various groups. The attributes most commonly used to classify foods seem to include dietary status of the population, food consumption patterns, availability, cost, and nutrient content (Ahlstrom and Rasanen, 1973; Hertzler and Anderson, 1974; Light and Cronin, 1981). Other attributes, however, also have been used. In their review of food grouping systems used in 47 countries, Ahlstrom and Rasanen (1973) provide examples of other criteria. In Finland, for example, use in food preparation and botanical criteria rather than vitamin content characterize food groups. In France, fruits and vegetables are divided into two groups--fresh fruits and vegetables and cooked fruits and vegetables.

Although researchers have listed attributes used to develop their food groups, they have omitted, for the most part, the actual rules that govern the assignment of an object (i.e., the food) to a class (i.e., the food group). In addition, none of the investigators have considered whether they are working in the classical, probabilistic, or exemplar mode of classification systems, which would affect the rules that they used implicitly or should have developed. Regardless of the viewpoint, two sets of rules are needed to develop a food classification system. The first set decides what objects (i.e., foods) should be included in the classification system. The second set determines the distribution of these objects among the groups. To illustrate, let's take the commonly used attributes, food consumption patterns and nutrient content. First, a set of rules must be developed to decide what foods will be included in the classification system. For this step, the most appropriate attribute seems to be food consumption patterns--that is, our objective could be to include the foods most commonly eaten by Americans. Thus, a rule must be developed that defines "most commonly eaten foods." One rule could be that a food will be included in the classification system only if 20% of the population ate it at least once in a one-week period. (Obviously, a number of variations on this rule can be developed.) The application of this rule results in the universe of foods to be included in the classification system.

Given our universe of foods, the second set of rules must be developed so that 1) appropriate groups can be determined, and 2) the foods within the universe can be assigned to a group. For this step, the most appropriate attribute seems to be nutrient content. Ostensibly, the first rule would concern which nutrients should be used. A commonly used rule is the "problem nutrient rule." This rule says that the nutrients or dietary constituents low in the American diet are considered to be the most important attributes (Note: defining what is meant by "low" is another rule.) Thus, if a certain nutrient or dietary constituent is low in the diet, then a group must be used to convey the use of this nutrient. For example, let's say that the American diet has been determined to be low in dietary fiber. At least one group then should be developed to convey the use of this dietary constituent--e.g., a plant group. Once the groups are developed, the next step would be to develop the rules for food assignment to the various groups. One rule might address the level at which a nutrient or dietary constituent must be present (or in combination with other nutrients) to be placed in a group.

From this very basic description on how to develop a classification system, one can see how complicated it can become very quickly with the number of foods and nutrients that must be considered. This example does not even include some of the other attributes that might be relevant like food cost or convenience in preparation.

As stated previously, most creators of food guides generally omit the rules for development and evaluation of the classification system of their guides, even though they go to great lengths to state explicitly the criteria used for the development and evaluation of the guidance component. Only one example can be found of a food guide for which the criteria used for the classification component were developed to some degree. Dodds (1981) presented six criteria on which she based her Handy Five Food guide. Only one of the criteria, must meet nutritional needs, is related to the guidance component; the remaining five criteria are related to the classification component of her food guide. Of these five, two established the rules for inclusion of foods into the classification system. Namely, the foods included in the universe would be 1) economical foods which best support health and 2) only a small number of groups should be used so that the classification system could be easily displayed and remembered. Lastly, the rule for assignment of foods into groups was based on characteristics that were observable (animal and plant parts) rather than abstract (nutrient composition). Her classification system, like the name, has five food groups characterized by animal and plant parts: 1) flesh around seeds (fruits), 2) leaves, stalks, roots, flowers (vegetables), 3) seeds on grasses (grains), 4) seeds in pods (nuts and legumes), and 5) animal products.

The usability of food guides by consumers has been an issue frequently raised by critics. One criticism is that the food guides use food groups that do not reflect consumers' classification systems. To date, Axelson, Kurinij, and Brinberg (1986) have conducted the only study which has tried to test whether the food groupings represented by a food guide reflect consumers' classification system. Their study addressed two questions: If individuals are given foods representative of the Four Food Groups (USDA, 1957), how would they group the foods? And, given the individuals' food classification system, what are the underlying dimensions (attributes) on which the individuals group the foods?

To answer the first question, a multivariate technique called multidimensional scaling (MDS), was used. MDS is an analytical procedure which can provide a visual display of the respondents' grouping of objects, even when the attributes on which similarity judgments made by respondents are unknown to the investigator. Respondents were given all possible pairs of 23 foods (253 pairs) and asked to judge the perceived similarity of each food pair on an 11-point scale ranging from extremely similar to extremely dissimilar. Using these similarity judgments, a cognitive "map" of respondents' food groups was obtained. On a cognitive map, the closer two objects (i.e., foods), the more similar the respondents perceive them to be. According to the cognitive map, ice cream, yogurt, milk, cheese, eggs, and peanut butter seemed to form a group which contain foods mostly from the Milk group. Flounder, chicken, roast beef, hamburger, hot dogs, and bacon clustered together and are all from the Meat group. (Note: bacon is placed in the Meat group in the Four Food Groups guide.) Doughnuts and bread (white and whole wheat) grouped together to form the Bread-cereals group. Carrots, tomatoes, and broccoli, with corn and oranges on the periphery, seemed to form the Fruit-vegetable group. In addition, rice, French-fried potatoes, and navy beans seemed to form a cluster which could be a high-starch group. Thus, the respondents seemed to group foods in a manner related to but more complex than the Four Food Groups. Some foods like eggs, peanut butter, and navy beans, which are meat substitutes were not placed in the Meat group. Furthermore, there may be additional groups in their classification system like a high-starch group.

To answer the second question of what are the underlying attributes on which the individuals grouped the foods, respondents were asked to rate each of the 23 foods on 21 scales. Thirteen of the scales were anchored with bipolar adjectives or phrases like good for your health/bad for your health, slimming/fattening, and feminine/masculine. The other eight were nutrient scales on which respondents rated the food as being either a poor, fair, good, or excellent source of vitamin A, vitamin C, protein, fat, carbohydrate, calcium, iron, and dietary fiber. The results of this analysis indicated that the respondents seemed to have perceived similarities among food based on three dimensions--convenience in preparation, health-related properties, and source (animal and plant). In addition, four of the eight nutrients seemed to be related to the three dimensions, indicating that nutrient composition of foods may be an attribute used by respondents to group foods. Axelson *et al.* (1986) concluded that the Four Food Groups guide is not entirely unlike the respondents' food classification system, but it probably needs to be expanded to include more groups (e.g., a legumes group) as well as modified to consider consumers' perceptions of foods' attributes (e.g., not having both animal and plant products in one group).

Consumers' Classification Systems

> "One of the outstanding difficulties in analyzing data about foods is to find categories which have meaning from the nutritionist's point of view and still are in line with the everyday terms in which the housewife thinks and acts. The thinking of the housewife is guided by quite a variety of aspects such as health, money, food for husband, breakfast foods, food for Thanksgiving, etc. It seems to be impossible to get a perfect classification system which takes in all these aspects at once. We have followed a line which, on the whole, tries to keep close to the thinking of the housewife." (Lewin, 1943, pg 36)

Lewin in 1943 succinctly states the central problem with food classification systems--namely, the problem of finding a food grouping system that is meaningful to food and nutrition professionals as well as individuals in the general population. Schutz and coworkers (1975) have criticized food classification systems developed by professionals on the grounds that the systems tend to reflect the professionals' perceptions of food groupings rather than the food users' groupings. If the two systems are substantially different, then food guides developed by nutritionists may be ineffective tools for nutrition educators because those guides are inconsistent with people's perceptions of foods. On the other hand, if professionals and the public use similar groups, then the next question would be--do they use the same attributes in their summary descriptions of the food groups? If these summary descriptions are not similar, then again there is the potential problem of poor communication because nutritionists may use a food group thinking that they are conveying a certain set of ideas, but the consumers may misunderstand the message because they perceive the group in an entirely different manner.

Issues involved in the elucidation of individuals' food classification systems are similar to those involved in the development of food classification systems for the cognitive component of food guides. One issue is what constitutes an object for classification; meaning, at what level is an object processed and classified by an individual? For example, do people think of "macaroni and cheese" as an object which can classified, or do they think of it in terms of one component like "cheese" which can be classified, or do they break this food into two components "macaroni" and "cheese" before classifying it? Or, do people think of "milk" as an object, or do they break it down into smaller units such as "calcium" and "protein" before attempting a classification? The answer to this issue governs the level at which objects should be presented to respondents for classification. Furthermore, the level at which individuals think of objects will affect directly the types of classes used in the final food classification system. If people think of objects at different levels [e.g., proteins (food constituent), apples (food item), and macaroni and cheese (food mixture)], then the classification system should probably reflect their thinking by the types of classes in the system.

Lewin (1943, pg 35) undertook a study to investigate "some aspects of why people eat what they eat." And like most researchers that want to examine food consumption and its relationship to other variables, he found the task of categorizing foods into meaningful groups difficult (refer to Lewin's quote). After acknowledging the difficulty of the task, he listed his categories without further explanation. His 25 categories were bread (bread, rolls, buns, biscuits; does not include toast); butter; casserole (includes foods frequently prepared in a casserole, as spaghetti and macaroni); caffeines (coffee, tea, coca cola); cereal (dry and cooked); cheese; desserts (pies, puddings, custards, cakes, etc.); eggs; fish; flour; fowl; fruit; fruit juices; leftovers; meat (excluding fowl); milk (includes milk, butter-milk, cocoa, chocolate milk); potatoes; relishes (includes mustard, ketchup, other seasoning, pickles, spiced fruits and vegetables); salads (fruit and vegetable salads); sandwiches; shortening; soup; sweets; toast; vegetables (including tomatoes but not potatoes). His list includes several types of classes: foods (i.e., butter, eggs, potatoes, shortening, toast); food groups (i.e., breads, cereal, cheese, fish, flour, fowl, fruit, fruit juices, meat, milk, vegetables); food constituents (caffeines, sweets); food-use groups (i.e., relishes, desserts); and food mixtures (i.e., salads, sandwiches, soup).

The other issue focuses on which attributes people use in their summary descriptions of food classes? For example, some attributes of milk are 1) it's white, 2) it's an animal product, 3) it can be used in coffee, 4) it can be used with a cereal, 5) it is a good source of calcium, and so forth. The question is which attribute or combination of attributes do people use to describe and classify the food into a group? The attribute of white might not be important, but the attribute, animal product, might be. This issue relates to what concepts are conveyed when using a particular food class in the cognitive component of a food guide.

The investigation into people's food classification systems is rather fragmentary and rudimentary. This statement reflects the state of knowledge and is not a criticism of the researchers and their efforts. These researchers face a formidable task because, without efforts from previous investigations, they have little but their own intuitions from which to start. Most of the research done seems to reflect a probabilistic point of view in that summary descriptions of food classes are used and that these descriptions are comprised of prominent attributes (features and dimensions) which have a substantial probability of occurring. Virtually no one, however, starts from a theoretical base that relates directly to the food classification systems found in the more popular food guides. Thus, most do not have any theoretical base for choosing the foods that they ask respondents to classify (and we will see that most investigators often do not state any reason for choosing the foods that they use in their investigations). Without a theoretical base as to the manner in which people structure their perceptions of foods, researchers can make no *a priori* predictions which they can test. Similarly, researchers often do not have any theoretical reasons for choosing the attributes on which they ask respondents to rate foods. For these reasons, the research can be called exploratory and descriptive.

Some investigations concerning the food classification systems of populations have been undertaken with the assumption that an understanding of the general population's food classification systems needs to be obtained before a meaningful system for everyone can be developed. Even though most of these studies do not have the explicit objective of evaluating the classification component of food guides, they are worth examining for two reason: 1) they may demonstrate some techniques that are applicable to studying the classification systems of food guides, and 2) the results may shed some light on consumers' perceptions of food classes and the attributes on which people classify foods.

Techniques. For the most part, investigators have used three techniques--factor analysis, cluster analysis, and multidimensional scaling--to examine consumers' food groupings. What all these techniques have in common is that they are multivariate statistical techniques which allow the investigators to reduce a large number of variables (e.g., foods) into a smaller set (i.e., groups) of variables. These techniques are used when the investigators hypothesize (or at least have a hunch) that there are some variables in the data set that are more interrelated than others--that is, the investigators believe that there are meaningful groupings of variables. Each of these techniques really represents a category of approaches. A quick sketch of the fundamentals of each type of analysis should provide the reader with enough information to understand the research in the area.

Factor analysis involves two steps: 1) collecting the information to form the data matrix, and 2) analyzing the data matrix to find the factors (i.e., the group of interrelated variables) (Nunnally, 1978). The data matrix will be a persons (rows) by variables (columns) table. For example, you may ask 100 people to rate six foods (e.g., ice cream, chocolate bar, cookies, apples, broccoli, and tomatoes) on a 9-point scale, ranging from good for you to bad for you. From this data matrix, factors are derived from linear combinations of the variables. Each factor is thought of as sharing a common source of variance among the variables. To examine how each factor accounts for a certain proportion of the variance of each variable, the matrix of factor loadings is examined. For example, Table 7.2 is a hypothetical matrix of factor loadings of our data from a principal component analysis with a Varimax (orthogonal) rotation.

The factor loadings in Table 7.2 indicate the relationship of each variable with each factor. Factor loadings can be seen as correlation coefficients between the variable and the factor; for example, the correlation between ice cream and Factor 1 is 0.85. And, like any correlation coefficient, the higher it is, the greater the strength of the relationship. (Note: factor loadings that are less than 0.50 are usually considered weak.) The proportion of variance explained by a factor

Table 7.2
Matrix of Factor Loadings

Variable	Factors	
	1	2
Ice cream	.85	.15
Chocolate bar	.92	.04
Cookies	.73	.09
Apples	.01	.88
Broccoli	.19	.77
Tomatoes	.11	.69
Sum of squared loadings	2.15	1.87
Variance, percent	35.8	31.3

for a particular variable can be determined by squaring the particular factor loading. For the variable ice cream, Factor 1 explains 75% of the variance (0.85 squared times 100 = % variance). The total amount of variance explained by any factor for the group of variables is the sum of squares of their factor loadings. From this sum of squared loadings (e.g., 2.15), the percent variance explained by the factor is obtained by dividing it (2.15) by the number of variables and multiplying by 100 (2.15/6 times 100 = 35.8%). Examining the pattern of factor loadings, it seems that ice cream, chocolate bar, and cookies all load significantly on Factor 1, and oranges, broccoli, and tomatoes load significantly on Factor 2. At this point, it is up to the investigator to interpret the factors. The investigator would examine the objects that loaded the highest on each factor and try to discern what attributes they had in common. In this case, Factor 1 could be interpreted as a dessert or sweet foods factor, and Factor 2 as a fruit and vegetables factor.

Factor analysis is a powerful statistical tool by which to examine the interrelationships among variables; however, there is one disadvantage when using factor analysis to examine the relationships among foods. Each food must be rated by individuals on at least one attribute, which means the investigator must choose an attribute on which to base the analysis. The investigator, however, may not know which attribute(s) is the most relevant.

Multidimensional scaling (MDS) is a technique which can overcome this disadvantage. MDS is an analytical procedure which can provide a visual display of the respondents' grouping of objects, even when the attributes (dimensions) on which similarity judgments made by the respondents are unknown to the investigator (Schiffman, Reynolds, & Young, 1981). In a MDS analysis, respondents usually are not asked to make responses with respect to a particular attribute, but rather they are asked to rate objects with respect to how similar or dissimilar they are. Objects (e.g., foods) that are perceived as similar will be closer together, and those that are perceived as dissimilar will be further apart on the visual display (map). Returning to our example, respondents would be asked to rate all possible pairs of the six foods (15 combinations like ice cream-tomato) on a similar/dissimilar scale. In this case, a MDS analysis could result in a one-dimensional solution with the foods grouping at opposite ends of the dimension (Figure 7.1).

ice cream		broccoli	
chocolate bar	tomatoes		apples
cookies			

Fig. 7.1. Hypothetical one-dimensional MDS solution.

Once the map of the foods (objects) is obtained, the investigator will attempt to interpret the dimension(s) by having the respondents rate each of the foods on a series of attribute scales which then can be regressed on the dimension(s). The results of the regression analysis facilitate interpretation of the dimension(s). For this example, the investigator might interpret the dimension as a "foods that are good for you/foods that are bad for you" dimension.

MDS is an effective technique for identifying respondents' implicit groupings of foods (objects) because the researcher does not need 1) to impose certain attributes on the respondents or 2) to have *a priori* knowledge about the attributes respondents will use to make similarity judgments. The main disadvantage of most MDS techniques is that only a limited number of foods (objects) can be included because all possible pairs of foods must be judged, and the number of judgments required can become unreasonable. For example, 25 foods would require 300 judgments, 30 foods 435 judgments, and 50 foods 1,225 judgments.

Cluster analysis is a group of techniques designed to classify variables into clusters (groups) that consist of variables that are related highly with one another, but have comparatively low relationships with variables in other clusters (Nunnally, 1978). Dillon and Goldstein (1984) outline the four basic steps needed to perform a cluster analysis. First, data are collected on the characteristics of the objects. Going back to the previous example used for the factor analysis, respondents could be asked to rate the six foods (objects) on a characteristic like good for you/bad for you. Second, this data matrix (objects x attribute) is transformed into a similarity matrix. This matrix has all of the objects listed in the rows as well as the columns, and placed in the matrix are distances between the objects based on computations from the attribute measurements. Third, the objects are clustered by using the similarity matrix, or distances between the objects. There are a number of available algorithms (formulas) which can be used to perform the cluster analysis. Last, the objects in each cluster are compared to the objects in other clusters by examining the mean values on the attributes of interest. If we cluster analyzed our data set, we might find two clusters: one being the ice cream, chocolate bar, and cookies, and the second cluster comprised of the apples, broccoli, and tomatoes.

From this description of cluster analysis, it can be seen that it can be used to analyze data that were collected for use with factor analysis or it can be used to analyze data that were collected for use with MDS. If a data matrix has an object-by-attribute measurement like those used in factor analysis, then there are two disadvantages of using cluster analysis: first, the difficulty with deciding the appropriate attribute(s) to use; second, the data matrix must be transformed into a similarity matrix. There are a number of algorithms for this transformation; however, Aldenderfer and Blashfield (1984) point out that different methods often result in different similarity values in the matrix. On the other hand, with a data set to be used with MDS, you already have a similarity matrix, so you start with step two in cluster analysis, but you have the disadvantages already cited for MDS techniques. There are two important problems (among others) with cluster analysis, according to Aldenderfer and Blashfield (1984). One is that there are a number of different clustering techniques and each of these techniques can give you different solutions, even when using the same data set. When it is appropriate to use the various techniques has not been worked out. A second problem is that there are not any well-developed techniques to determine the number of "natural" clusters in a data set. In contrast, factor analysis and MDS have some methods (or good rules of thumb) by which to determine how many factors or dimensions seem to best describe the data.

These three multivariate techniques have two disadvantages in common. First, once the factor, map, or cluster is obtained, the burden of interpretation as to the attribute(s) which the grouped objects have in common falls on the investigator. Second, the factor, map, or cluster could change if other foods (objects) had been included because the resultant structures are based on the actual objects judged by the respondents.

<u>Research</u>. Investigators besides those involved in the development of food guides have given some thought to people's classifica-

tion of foods. Generally, two approaches to this topic have been taken. The first approach is one where investigators try to understand people's perceptions (categories) of food by reflecting on the role food plays in society and reporting their thoughts. The second approach is one where the investigators directly ask respondents about their food perceptions. This task is accomplished in one of two ways. First, investigators ask respondents to categorize foods on one or more attributes given by the researcher. The assumption in this type of study is that the important attribute(s) which respondents use to classify foods has been chosen, and thus the resulting food groups reflect their "natural" classification system. Second, investigators give respondents a list of foods in some form and ask them to group the foods using any attributes they wish. The rationale for this approach is not to contaminate the respondents with the investigators' attributes, but to allow respondents to present their own "natural" food classification system. This task is often followed by asking the respondents about the reasons (attributes) for their groupings.

Examples of the first approach include work done by Jelliffe (1967) and Leininger (1969). Both Jelliffe and Leininger characterize the "reflect and report your thoughts" approach to understanding food classification systems. This approach seems to be the dominant one until the 1970s. The following comment by Jelliffe (1967, pg 279) indicates the basis for his classification system:

> "Innumerable systems of classification can be made, but the following five are arbitrarily considered here because they appear to be world-wide, affecting both developing and industrialized regions, and also because they are often of importance to the public health nutritionist."

Jelliffe's five classes of food are 1) cultural superfoods--these items are mainly the predominant staple defined as the major source of calories; 2) prestige foods--these items (mostly animal products) are reserved for special occasions and prominent members of the community; 3) body-image foods--these items are eaten or avoided depending on state of health; 4) sympathetic magic foods--these items are eaten or avoided because a property of the food is thought to translate into a property of the body, e.g., an athlete may eat meat (a muscle) to build muscles; and 5) physiologic group foods--these items are eaten or avoided by certain physiologic groups based on age, gender, or status like pregnancy. In a similar manner, Leininger (1969, pg 154) tried to "identify some of the universal and non-universal functions, beliefs, and practices of food cross-culturally." She identified nine universal uses of foods: 1) satisfaction of biophysiological hunger, 2) initiation and maintenance of interpersonal relationships, 3) definition of social distance among individuals, 4) expression of social and religious ideas, 5) acknowledgment of social status and achievement of an individual or group, 6) a means to cope with psychological stress and needs, 7) a reward or punishment, 8) instrument by which to affect the political and economic status of a group, and 9) a treatment for physical as well as social illnesses.

Although discussions like these are very thought-provoking, they provide little insight into the cognitive structure related to foods which an individual uses on a daily level to make decisions about which foods to consume. In an effort to overcome the limitations of the "reflect and report" approach to assessing individuals' food and food-use categories, some investigators have tried a more direct approach--asking people about their perceptions. Examples of the approach characterized by using one or more attributes are studies done by Schutz, Rucker, and Russell (1975), Sobal and Cassidy (1987), and Drewnowski (1985).

Schutz and his coworkers (1975) developed a type of instrument which allows investigators to examine foods in relationship to food-use attributes. This instrument is a matrix which has food uses (e.g., for dessert, with friends) in the columns and food items (e.g., milk, chop suey) in the rows. To complete this matrix, respondents evaluate all possible food and food use pairs on a 7-point scale ranging from never appropriate to always appropriate. For example, a respondent might evaluate "milk--for dessert" as never appropriate. The data from the completed matrices then are analyzed by using factor analytic techniques. The analysis can result in two grouping systems: food groups and food-use groups. Schutz and his co-workers have used this instrument in a number of studies (e.g., Bruhn and Schutz, 1986); however, only one will be reported here as an example.

Schutz, Rucker, and Russell (1975) used a wide range of foods (56 items) and situations (48 uses) in their food by food-use matrix. Two hundred women in four cities completed the questionnaire. No rationale was given for choosing the particular foods or situations included in the matrix. Five food factors (groups) and four food-use factors (groups) were found. The food groups were labeled: 1) high-calorie treat--included foods like wine, pie, and cake and were seen as most appropriate in situations like for guests and for special holidays; 2) specialty meal items--included foods like liver, chili, and chitterlings and were seen as inappropriate in most situations; 3) common meal items--included foods like chicken, roast beef, and steak and were seen as appropriate for dinner and as a main dish as well as among a number of other situations; 4) refreshing healthy foods--included foods like jello, cottage cheese, and orange juice and were seen as appropriate in summer and served cold; and 5) inexpensive filling foods--included foods like peanut butter, candy bars, and potato chips and were seen as appropriate for teenagers and for eating with fingers. The food-use groups were labeled: 1) utilitarian--included situations for teenagers, for children, and easy to prepare, and ice cream and frankfurters were seen best for these uses; 2) casual--included situations when unhappy, riding in a car, and not feeling well, and none of the foods included in the study were seen as especially appropriate for these situations, 3) satiating--included situations eating with a fork, as a main dish, and for dinner, and roast beef, steak, and spaghetti were seen as appropriate in these situations; and 4) social--included situations at parties, with friends, and for guests with dip, coffee, wine, and cake seen as appropriate foods.

This approach of examining food groups on the basis of the attribute of food use in particular situations results in food groupings that have differential relevance to the food and nutrition professional. Food groupings like "high-calorie treat" and "common meal items" are characterized by foods with similar compositions, but the "refreshing healthy" foods group which included foods like jello, cottage cheese, and orange juice would be a food group difficult to translate into behavioral recommendations, if included in the cognitive component of a food guide. As will be shown, there is evidence to indicate that individuals use other attributes in addition to food use to classify foods.

Sobal and Cassidy (1987) asked 374 undergraduate students, "If you had to name three dieting (weight loss) foods, what would they be?" The three most frequently mentioned items were vegetables (38% of the respondents), fruits, (36%), and salads (27%). The most frequently mentioned (60% of respondents) reason that these foods were considered dieting foods was "low in calories." These investigators stated that their objective was to assess whether the category of "dieting foods" existed as a "natural grouping in people's minds" (Sobal and Cassidy, 1987, pg 89). Their study design, however, does not allow this question to be answered unequivocally. First, the manner in which they asked the question seems to force a positive response, meaning it did not allow an option for no "dieting" foods. Second, even if the respondents would not have taken the negative option if provided, the investigators provide no criteria by which they decided that there was enough evidence to conclude there is a "natural grouping in people's minds." In other words, if some other attributes were used, would the same set of responses be obtained? For example, if some other group of undergraduates had been asked "to name three low-calorie foods" or "to name three healthful foods," would the response set be the same?

Drewnowski (1985) asked 38 obese and 35 normal weight subjects to judge "how different from each other in nutritional value" all possible pairs (n=120) of 16 foods (e.g., eggs) and food groups (e.g., fruits). Food items were selected from a questionnaire designed to assess maternal and child nutrition by a federal agency. The respondents also rated each of the 16 foods on five attribute scales: protein, fat, and carbohydrate content, and caloric and nutritional value. Respondents' perceived similarity among the foods were analyzed by using multidimensional scaling (MDS) and cluster analyses. The MDS analysis produced a two-dimensional solution (no differences between normal and obese subjects were found). Examining the visual display (map) of the two-dimensional solution, there appears to be at least five groups: 1) milk, eggs, and peanut butter, 2) fruit and vegetables, 3) cereals, macaroni, bread, and potatoes, 4) candy, soft drinks, cake, cookies, doughnuts, and potato chips, and 5) ice cream. (Note: this interpretation of food groups is ours and not Drewnowski's.) Using cluster analysis, Drewnowski grouped the foods into four groups: 1) healthy foods--eggs, milk, peanut butter, fruit, and vegetables, 2) starches--bread, cereals, macaroni, and potatoes, 3) snacks--candy, ice cream, and soft drinks, and 4) desserts--cakes, cookies, and doughnuts (potato chips were not mentioned). By regressing the respondents' responses on the five attribute scales onto the two dimensions, Drewnowski interpreted the first dimension as a nutritious versus a high-energy foods, and the second as a carbohydrate versus protein and fat dimension. Dividing the "map" into four quadrants and labeling the quadrants with the interpretations of the dimensions, the manner in which the attributes were perceived to be related to the foods can be found (Table 7.3).

As mentioned before, the assumption in this type of study where the respondents are asked to rate foods on attributes given by the investigators is that the attributes represent the ones which respondents would use to classify foods. In other words, the attributes would be part of the summary description used to represent a class of objects. Obviously, if the attributes given by the researcher are not the prominent ones used by individuals, then the food groupings based on these attributes may not reflect the most common system. An approach that tries to overcome this weakness is one where the investigator gives the respondents foods to categorize without giving them any attributes. Studies done by Campbell, Roe, and Eickwort (1982) and Michela and Contento (1984) serve as good examples of this approach.

Table 7.3
Relationship of Foods to Attributes from MDS Solution

Second Dimension Attributes	First Dimension Attributes	
	Nutritious	High-energy
Protein & fat	milk eggs peanut butter	ice cream
Carbohydrate	fruit vegetables cereals macaroni bread potatoes	candy soft drinks cake doughnuts potato chips cookies

As part of a larger study examining diet indexes, Campbell, Roe, and Eickwort (1982) studied food grouping systems of 194 women attending family planning clinics. Women were given pictures of 76 foods and asked to sort them into groups of foods that were similar to each other in some way. After sorting the pictures, each respondent was asked about her rationale for the grouping. These groupings were analyzed by cluster analysis. The respondents grouped the 76 foods into eight major categories or 18 smaller categories, depending on where the cutoff point was set in the cluster analysis. The respondents' groupings are presented in Table 7.4. Campbell and coworkers (1982) did not provide very much information about the respondents' rationale for these groupings; however, they did say that "78 percent of the sample grouped foods on the basis of meat, vegetable, fruit, dairy, and cereal type categories, there was a subgroup of older, less educated women who grouped the foods in terms of the degree of liking or disliking and/or when or how often they ate the food." Examining the groups in Table 7.4, they could be named 1) fruits, 2) vegetables, 3) breads, cereals, and potatoes (a high-starch group), 4) sweets and snacks, 5) dairy and eggs, 6) nonnutritive beverages, 7) meat, and 8) peanuts. This study represents a look at individuals' food classification systems using the most number of foods. But because it was not the objective of the authors, the attributes on which the respondents based their groupings were not examined closely.

Like Campbell *et al.* (1982), Michela and Contento (1984) examined individuals' food classification systems by using a large number of foods. Their respondents, however, were 115 children, aged 5 to 11. The children were given pictures of 71 foods and asked to group the foods by using their own criteria. They then were asked to label the groups that they created. The data were analyzed by cluster analysis and multidimensional scaling techniques. The results of the cluster analysis are given in Table 7.4. Only 40 of the 71 foods are shown because the researchers did not list all of them in the article. The food groupings of the women in Campbell *et al.*'s study and of the children in Michela and Contento's study are very similar. Michela and Contento (1984) reported that most of the children used traditional semantic categories like fruits, meats, and breads to describe their categories. The MDS analysis resulted in a four-dimensional solution. The researchers interpreted the dimensions in the following manner. Dimension 1 seemed to represent a classification based on sweet versus nonsweet foods. Dimension 2 seemed to distinguish foods based on physical characteristics, with meal entrees on one end of the dimension and drinks on the other end. (Note: our observation is that the foods go from solid to liquid or hard to soft.) Dimension 3 was interpreted as a whole, fresh, less processed foods

Table 7.4

Consumers' Food Classifications Based on Cluster Analysis

Authors	Groups		
Campbell, Roe, &	1	2	3
Eickwort, 1982[a]	1a	2a	3a
	apples	asparagus	bagels
	applesauce	beets	crackers
	apricots	broccoli	white bread
	bananas	cabbage	whole wheat
	grapefruit	carrots	bread
	oranges	cauliflower	
	pears	celery	3b
	pineapple	corn	corn flakes
	prunes	dried peas	oatmeal
	raisins	green beans	pancakes
	strawberries	lettuce	
	watermelon	lima beans	3c
		onions	noodles
	1b	peas	rice
	orange juice	squash	
		tomatoes	3d
			French fries
		2b	baked potatoes
		tomato	mashed potatoes
		juice	
			3e
			sweet potatoes
Michela &	Fruits	Vegetables	Breakfast Foods
Contento, 1984[b]			& Breads
	apple	beets	bagels
	watermelon	broccoli	cereal
		carrots	eggs
		corn	oatmeal
		green peas	waffles
		lima beans	
		potatoes	
		sweet potatoes	
		tomato	

[a]   Depending on the cutoff point specified, either 8 or 18 groups were found.

Groups				
4	5	6	7	8
4a	5a			
cakes	butter	beer	bacon	peanut butter
chocolate	cheese	coffee	bologna	peanuts
bar	cottage	pop	chicken	
cookies	cheese	wine	ham	
sweet roll	milk		hamburger	
			hot dog	
4b	5b		liver	
popcorn	ice cream		perch	
potato	milkshake		pork chops	
chips	whipping		steak	
	cream		tuna	
4c	yogurt			
jelly				
	5c			
	eggs			

Sweets	Cheese & Yogurt	Drinks	Meats	Mixed Foods
candy	cheese	milk	chicken	noodles
cake	yogurt	orange	fish	rice
cookies		juice	hot dog	sandwich
ice cream		soda	meat patty	spaghetti mix
jello			steak	soup
pretzels				tacos
Twinkies				salad

[b] The actual foods belonging to each cluster were not given entirely; this table is the result of some guesswork.

versus cooked, more highly processed foods; however, the authors think that this distinction is too advanced for the children. (Note: another interpretation of this dimension could be based on the physical characteristics of juicy versus dry.) The fourth dimension was interpreted as animal versus plant foods.

In summary, food classification systems are used by both nutrition professionals and individuals in the general population to organize and communicate information. Professionals have developed food guides to communicate nutrition information to the public. These guides can be divided into two components: 1) the classification component--usually some groupings of food--provides the cognitive structure which is used to communicate basic concepts, and 2) the guidance component--usually a suggested number of servings from each group in the classification system--provides the specific behaviors which individuals should undertake to comply with the information given in the classification system.

One major criticism of most currently used food guides is that they are ineffective communication tools. Generally, two reasons for this observation are given. First, critics claim that many of the classification systems do not communicate the intended message. For example, both Pennington (1981) and Lachance (1981) suggest that the manner in which food groups are presented does not reflect the recommended levels of consumption. Second, critics claim that the classification systems contained in the commonly used food guides reflect the professionals' perceptions of food groupings rather than the consumers' perceptions and that this lack of fit between the two systems results in poor communication of nutrition-related concepts to consumers.

At this time, the charges of the critics cannot be answered. The classification component of the food guides has been inadequately tested, and consumers' perceptions of food groupings have not been adequately studied. One important question that needs to be studied is the level at which individuals process and classify objects. Apples, steak, and cheese seem to be examples of objects that are classified at the level which most people would call a food item; however, many foods like macaroni and cheese are food mixtures. Thus, are food mixtures considered an object for classification or does one component of the mixture act as the object for classification?

Another important issue involves discerning individuals' "natural" food groupings. A number of studies (e.g., Axelson, Kurinij, and Brinberg, 1986; Campbell, Roe, and Eickwort, 1982; Michela & Contento, 1984) indicate that there seem to be some food groupings that are understood and used by members of the US population. Examples of these commonly understood groupings are fruits, vegetables, and meats. Some food groupings that are used in food guides, however, are not discerned easily in studies of consumers' food perceptions. For example, both Axelson and coworkers (1986) and Drewnowski (1985) found that peanut butter and eggs grouped with milk products. Similarly, Campbell *et al.* (1982) found that eggs grouped with dairy products, but peanuts and peanut butter formed a separate group. Another group traditionally used in food guides is breads and cereals. Campbell *et al.* (1982) found that potatoes were included in this group; however, Michela & Contento (1984) found that potatoes clustered with the vegetables. To complicate the picture, Axelson *et al.* (1986) found, in addition to a breads group, a high-starch group which included rice, potatoes, and navy beans. The grouping of food mixtures has been virtually ignored, except by Michela & Contento (1984).

To fully understand individuals' food grouping systems, the prominent attributes (summary description) which define the foods in a group must be examined. As mentioned before, food groups are used in food guides to convey information. When the nutrition professionals' summary descriptions of the food groups conflict with the intended audiences' summary descriptions, there is a greater probability that the nutrition message will not be well received or understood. For example, if "low in calories" is an important attribute of fruits, then the nutritionist might make a decision about whether to add another attribute like "high in dietary fiber" when presenting information to the group. The nutrition educator might decide that dietary fiber is not a dietary problem of the group, but obesity is; therefore, the best strategy would be to stay with the calories-related attribute.

A better understanding of consumers' food classification systems is needed. With a clearer picture of individuals' cognitive structures related to food and food use, professionals should be able to develop groupings which consumers understand and which are compatible with the goal of nutrition educators--to guide individuals in selecting health-promoting diets.

References

Abdel-Ghany, M., and Foster, A.C. (1982). Impact of income and wife's education on family consumption expenditures. *Journal of Consumer Studies and Home Economics* 6, 21-28.

Abdel-Ghany, M., and Schrimper, R.A. (1978). Food consumption expenditures and education of the homemaker. *Home Economics Research Journal* 6, 283-292.

Achterberg, C. (1988). A perspective on nutrition education research and practice. *Journal of Nutrition Education* 20(5), 240-243.

Adrian, J., and Daniel, R. (1976). Impact of socioeconomic factors on consumption of selected food nutrients in the United States. *American Journal of Agricultural Economics* 58, 31-38.

Ahlstrom, A., and Rasanen, L (1973). Review of food grouping systems in nutrition education. *Journal of Nutrition Education* 5, 13-17.

Ajzen, I., and Fishbein, M. (1980). *Understanding attitudes and predicting social behavior.* Englewood Cliffs, NJ: Prentice-Hall, Inc.

Akin, J.S., Guilkey, D.K., Popkin, B.M., and Fanelli, M.T. (1986). Cluster analysis of food consumption patterns of older Americans. *Journal of The American Dietetics Association* 86, 616-624.

Aldenderfer, M.S., and Blashfield, R.K. (1984). *Cluster analysis.* Beverly Hills, CA: Sage Publications.

Anderson, N.A. (1981). *Foundations of information integration theory.* New York: Academic Press.

Axelson, J.M. (1977). *Food habits of North Florida teenagers: Their food preferences, meal patterns, and food and nutrition intakes.* Tallahassee, FL: Florida A & M University.

Axelson, M.L., Brinberg, D., and Durand, J.H. (1983). Eating at a fast-food restaurant--A social-psychological analysis. *Journal of Nutrition Education* 15, 94-98.

Axelson, M.L., Federline, T.L., and Brinberg, D. (1985). A meta-analysis of food- and nutrition-related research. *Journal of Nutrition Education* 17, 51-54.

Axelson, M.L., Kurinij, N., and Brinberg, D. (1986). An analysis of the Four Food Groups using multidimensional scaling. *Journal of Nutrition Education* 18, 265-273.

Baird, P.C., and Schutz, H.G. (1976). The marketing concept applied to "selling" good nutrition. *Journal of Nutrition Education* 8(1), 13-17.

Baird, P.C., and Schutz, H.G. (1980). Life style correlates of dietary and biochemical measures of nutrition. *Journal of The American Dietetic Association* 76, 228-235.

Barker, L.M. (ed.) (1982). *The psychobiology of human food selection.* Westport, CT: Avi Publishing Co.

Basiotis, P.P., Welsh, S.O., Cronin, F.J., Kelsay, J.L., and Mertz, W. (1987). Number of days of food intake records required to estimate individual and group nutrient intakes with defined confidence. *Journal of Nutrition* 117, 1638-1641.

Bayton, J.A. (1966). Problems of communication of nutrition information. In *National nutrition conference proceedings*, Misc. Publ. No. 1075. Washington, D.C.: U.S. Department of Agriculture.

Bazzarre, T.L., Yuhas, J.A., and Wu, S-M.L. (1983). Measures of food intake among rural elderly. *Journal of Nutrition for the Elderly* 2(4), 3-15.

Bettman, J.R., Capon, N., and Lutz, R.J. (1975). Cognitive algebra in multi-attribute attitude models. *Journal of Marketing Research* 12, 151-164.

Birch, L.L. (1979). Preschool children's food preferences and consumption patterns. *Journal of Nutrition Education* 11, 189-192.

Birch, L.L. (1980a). Effects of peer models' food choices and eating behaviors on preschoolers' food preferences. *Child Development* 51, 489-496.

Birch, L.L. (1980b). The relationship between children's food preferences and those of their parents. *Journal of Nutrition Education* 12, 14-18.

Birch, L.L. (1987). The role of experience in children's food acceptance patterns. *Journal of The American Dietetic Association* 87(9 supp.), S36-S40.

Birch, L.L., Birch, D., Marlin, D.W., and Kramer, L. (1982). Effects of instrumental consumption on children's food preference. *Appetite* 3, 125-134.

Blanciforti, L., Green, R., and Lane, S. (1981). Income and expenditures for relatively more versus relatively less nutritious food over the life cycle. *American Journal of Agricultural Economics* 63, 255-260.

Brinberg, D. (1979). An examination of the determinants of intention and behavior: A comparison of two models. *Journal of Applied Social Psychology* 9(6), 560-575.

Brinberg, D., and Durand, J. (1983). Eating at fast-food restaurants: An analysis using two behavioral intention models. *Journal of Applied Social Psychology* 13(6), 459-472.

Brinberg, D., and Jaccard, J. (1986). Meta-analysis: Techniques for the quantitative integration of research findings. In *Perspectives on methodology in consumer research*, pp. 155-180. D. Brinberg, R.J. Lutz (eds). New York: Springer-Verlag.

Brinberg, D., and Jaccard, J. (1989). Multiple perspectives on dyadic decision making. In *Dyadic decision making*, pp. 313-334. D. Brinberg, J. Jaccard (eds). New York: Springer-Verlag.

Brinberg, D., and McGrath, J.E. (1985). *Validity and the research process.* Beverly Hills, CA: Sage Publications.

Brittin, H.C., and Zinn, D.W. (1977). Meat-buying practices of Caucasians, Mexican-Americans, and Negroes. *Journal of The American Dietetic Association* 71, 623-628.

Bruhn, C.M., and Schutz, H.G. (1986). Consumer perceptions of dairy and related-use foods. *Food Technology* 40(1), 79-86.

Brunswik, E. (1955). Representative design and probabilistic theory in a functional psychology. *Psychological Review* 62, 193-217.

Burk, M.C., and Pao, E.M. (1976). *Methodology for large-scale surveys of household and individual diets.* Home Economics Research Report, No. 40. Washington D.C.: U.S. Department of Agriculture.

Byrd-Bredbenner, C., and Shear, T. (1982). Nutrition knowledge, attitude, dietary behavior, and commitment to nutrition education of nutrition educators. *Home Economics Research Journal* 11, 167-174.

Caliendo, M.A., and Sanjur, D. (1978). The dietary status of preschool children: An ecological approach. *Journal of Nutrition Education* 10, 69-72.

Campbell, C., Roe, D.A., and Eickwort, K. (1982). Qualitative diet indexes: A descriptive or an assessment tool? *Journal of The American Dietetic Association* 81, 687-694.

Campbell, D.T., and Fiske, D.W. (1959). Convergent and discriminant validation by the multitrait-multimethod matrix. *Psychological Bulletin* 56, 81-105.

Cardello, A.V., and Maller, O. (1982). Relationships between food preferences and food acceptance ratings. *Journal of Food Science* 47, 1553-1557, 1561.

Carter, R.L., Sharbaugh, C.O., and Stapell, C.A. (1981). Reliability and validity of the 24-hour recall. *Journal of The American Dietetic Association* 79, 542-551.

Caster, W.O., (1980). The core diet of lower-economic class women in Georgia. *Ecology of Food and Nutrition* 9, 241-246.

Contento, I.R., Michela, J.L., and Goldberg, C.J. (1988). Food choice among adolescents: Population segmentation by motivations. *Journal of Nutrition Education* 20, 289-298.

Cote, J.A., McCullough, J., and Reilly, M. (1985). Effects of unexpected situations on behavior-intention differences: A garbology analysis. *Journal of Consumer Research* 12, 188-194.

Cowart, B.J. (1981). Development of taste perception in humans: Sensitivity and preference throughout the life span. *Psychological Bulletin* 90(1), 43-73.

Cronbach, L.J., Gleser, G.C., Nanda, H., and Rajaratnam, N. (1972). *The dependability of behavioral measures: Theory of generalizability for scores and profiles.* New York: John Wiley Co.

Cronbach, L.J., Rajaratnam, N., and Gleser, G.C. (1963). Theory of generalization: A liberalization of reliability theory. *British Journal of Statistical Psychology* 16, 137-163.

Cronin, F.J., Krebs-Smith, S.M., Wyse, B.W., and Light, L. (1982). Characterizing food usage by demographic variables. *Journal of The American Dietetics Association* 81, 661-673.

Cronin, F.J., Shaw, A.M., Krebs-Smith, S.M., Marsland, P.M., and Light, L. (1987). Developing a food guidance system to implement the Dietary Guidelines. *Journal of Nutrition Education* 19, 281-302.

Davis, C.G. (1982) Linkages between socioeconomic characteristics, food expenditure patterns, and nutritional status of low income households: A critical review. *American Journal of Agricultural Economics* 64, 1017-1025.

Dennis, B., and Shifflett, P.A. (1985). A conceptual and methodological model for studying dietary habits in the community. *Ecology of Food and Nutrition* 17, 253-262.

Dewey, K.G., Strode, M.A., and Fitch, Y. (1984). Dietary change among migrant and nonmigrant Mexican-American families in northern California. *Ecology of Food and Nutrition* 14, 11-24.

Dillon, W.R., and Goldstein, M. (1984). *Multivariate analysis: Methods and applications.* New York: John Wiley and Sons.

Dillon, W.R., Madden, T.J., and Firtle, N.H. (1987). *Marketing research in a marketing environment.* St. Louis: Times Mirror/Mosby College Publishing.

Dodds, J.M. (1981). The Handy Five Food guide. *Journal of Nutrition Education* 13, 50-52.

Drewnowski, A. (1985). Food perceptions and preferences of obese adults: A multidimensional approach. *International Journal of Obesity* 9, 201-212.

Dwyer, J.T., Krall, E.A., and Coleman, K.A. (1987). The problem of memory in nutritional epidemiology research. *Journal of The American Dietetics Association* 87, 1509-1512.

Edwards, A.L. (1957). *Techniques of attitude scale construction.* New York: Appleton-Century-Crofts.

Einstein, M.A., and Hornstein, I. (1970). Food preferences of college students and nutritional implications. *Journal of Food Science* 35, 429-436.

Engen, T. (1986). Children's sense of smell. In *Clinical measurement of taste and smell,* pp. 316-325. H.L. Meiselman, R.S. Rivlin (eds). New York, NY: MacMillan Publishing Co.

Eppright, E.S., Fox, H.M., Fryer, B.A., Lamkin, G.H., and Vivian, V.M. (1970). The North Central Regional Study of diets of preschool children. 2. Nutrition knowledge and attitudes of mothers. *Journal of Home Economics* 62, 327-332.

Feldman, R.H.L., and Mayhew, P.C. (1984). Predicting nutrition behavior: The utilization of a social psychological model of health behavior. *Basic and Applied Social Psychology* 5(3), 183-195.

Fewster, W.J., Bostian, L.R., and Powers, R.D. (1973). Measuring the connotative meanings of foods. *Home Economics Research Journal* 2(1), 44-53.

Fishbein, M., and Ajzen, I. (1975). *Belief, attitude, intention, and behavior: An introduction to theory and research.* Reading, MA: Addison-Wesley Publishing Co.

Freedman, M.R., and Grivetti, L.E. (1984). Diet patterns of first, second, and third generation Greek-American women. *Ecology of Food and Nutrition* 14, 185-204.

Garcia, P.A., Battese, G.E., and Brewer, W.D. (1975). Longitudinal study of age and cohort influences on dietary practices. *Journal of Gerontology* 30, 349-356.

Gersovitz, M., Madden, J.P., and Smiciklas-Wright, H. (1978). Validity of the 24-hr. dietary recall and seven-day record for group comparisons. *Journal of The American Dietetics Association* 73, 48-55.

Glass, G.V., McGaw, B., and Smith, M.L. (1981). *Meta-analysis in social research.* Beverly Hills, CA: Sage Publications.

Goebel, K.P., and Hennon, C.B. (1982). An empirical investigation of the relationship among wife's employment status, stage in the family life cycle, meal preparation time, and expenditures for meals away from home. *Journal of Consumer Studies and Home Economics* 6, 63- 78.

Goebel, K.P., and Hennon, C.B. (1983). Mother's time on meal preparation, expenditures for meals away from home, and shared meals: Effects of mother's employment and age of younger child. *Home Economics Research Journal* 12, 169-188.

Grivetti, L.E., and Paquette, M.B. (1978). Nontraditional ethnic food choices among first generation Chinese in California. *Journal of Nutrition Education* 10, 109-112.

Grotkowski, M.L., and Sims, L.S. (1978). Nutritional knowledge, attitudes, and dietary practices of the elderly. *Journal of The American Dietetics Association* 72, 499-506.

Guthrie, J.F. (1988). Psychosocial determinants of consumption of fiber-rich foods. Unpublished Ph.D. dissertation, University of Maryland, College Park, MD.

Hafstrom, J.L., and Schram, V.R. (1983). Housework time of wives: Pressure, facilitators, constraints. *Home Economics Research Journal* 11, 245-255.

Hankin, J.H., Rhoads, G.G., and Glober, G.A. (1975). A dietary method for an epidemologic study of gastrointestinal cancer. *American Journal of Clinical Nutrition* 28, 1055-1061.

Haughton, B., Gussow, J.D., and Dodds, J.M. (1987). An historical study of the underlying assumptions for United States Food Guides from 1917 through the Basic Four Food Group Guide. *Journal of Nutrition Education* 19, 169-175.

Havlicek, J.Jr., Axelson, J.M., Capps, O.Jr., Pearson, J.M., and Richardson, S. (1983). Nutritional and economic aspects of convenience and nonconvenience foods. In *Proceedings of Outlook '83. Agricultural outlook conference*, pp. 539-550. Washington, D.C.: U.S. Department of Agriculture.

Heady, J.A. (1961). Diets of bank clerks--Development of a method of classifying the diets of individuals for use in epidemiological studies. *Journal of the Royal Statistical Society* 124, 336-361.

Hertzler, A.A., and Anderson, H.L. (1974). Food guides in the United States. *Journal of The American Dietetic Association* 64, 19-28.

Hinton, M.A., Eppright, E.S., Chadderon, H., and Wolins, L. (1963). Eating behavior and dietary intake of girls 12 to 14 years old. *Journal of The American Dietetic Association* 43, 223-227.

Hunt, W.C., Leonard, A.G., Garry, P.J., and Goodwin, J.S. (1983). Components of variance in dietary data for an elderly population. *Nutrition Research* 3, 433-444.

Immink, M.D.C., Sanjur, D., and Burgos, M. (1983). Nutritional consequences of U.S. migration patterns among Puerto Rican women. *Ecology of Food and Nutrition* 13, 139-148.

Jaccard, J., and Dittus, P. (in press). Idiographic and nomothetic perspectives on research methods and data analysis. In *Review of personality and social psychology*. C. Hendrick, M.S. Clark (eds). Newbury Park, CA: Sage Publications.

Jaccard, J., and King, G.W. (1977). The relation between behavioral intentions and beliefs: A probabilistic model. *Human Communication Research* 3(4), 326-334.

Jaccard, J., and Wood, G. (1986). An idiothetic analysis of behavioral decision making. In *Perspectives on methodology in consumer research*, pp. 67-106. D. Brinberg, R.J. Lutz (eds). New York: Springer-Verlag.

Jalso, S.B., Burns, M.M., and Rivers, J.M. (1965) Nutritional beliefs and practices. *Journal of The American Dietetic Association* 47, 263-268.

Jelliffe, D.B. (1967). Parallel food classifications in developing and industrialized countries. *American Journal of Clinical Nutrition* 20, 279-281.

Jerome, N.W. (1980). Diet and acculturation: The case of Black-American in-migrants. In *Nutritional anthropology. Contemporary approaches to diet and culture*, pp. 275-325. N. Jerome, R. Kandel, G. Pelto (eds). Pleasantville, NY: Redgrave.

Karkeck, J.M. (1987). Improving the use of dietary survey methodology. *Journal of The American Dietetic Association* 87, 869-871.

Kerlinger, F. (1973). *Foundations of behavioral research*. New York: Holt, Rinehart, and Winston.

King, G.A., Herman, C.P., and Polivy, J. (1987). Food perceptions in dieters and non-dieters. *Appetite* 8, 147-158.

King, J.C., Cohenour, S.H., Corruccini, C.G., and Schneeman, P. (1978). Evaluation and modification of the Basic Four Food guide. *Journal of Nutrition Education* 10, 27-29.

Klesges, R.C., Klesges, L.M., Brown, G., and Frank, G.C. (1987). Validation of the 24-hour dietary recall in preschool children. *Journal of The American Dietetics Association* 87, 1383-1385.

Krantzler, N.J., Mullen, B.J., Comstock, E.M., Holden, C.A., Schutz, H.G., Grivetti, L.E., and Meiselman, H.L. (1982). Methods of food intake assessment--An annotated bibliography. *Journal of Nutrition Education* 14(3), 108-119.

Lachance, P.A. (1981). A suggestion on food guides and dietary guidelines. *Journal of Nutrition Education* 13, 56.

Larson, R., and Csikszentmihalyi, M. (1983). The experiential sampling method. In *Naturalistic approaches to studying social interaction*, pp. 41-56. H.T. Reis (ed). San Francisco: Jossey-Bass.

Leininger, M. (1969). Some cross-cultural universal and non-universal functions, beliefs, and practices of food. In *Dimensions of nutrition*, pp. 153-179. J. Dupont (ed). Boulder, CO: Colorado Associated University Press.

Leonard, R.E. (1982). Nutrition profiles: Diets in the '80s. *The Community Nutritionist* 12-17.

Lewin, K. (1943). Forces behind food habits and methods of change. In *The problem of changing food habits. Report of the committee on food habits,* pp. 35-65. Bull. 108, Washington, D.C.: National Academy of Sciences.

Light, L., and Cronin, F.J. (1981). Food guidance revisited. *Journal of Nutrition Education* 13, 57-62.

Lippert, A., and Love, D.O. (1986). Family expenditures for food away from home and prepared foods. *Family Economics Review* 3, 9-14.

Logue, A.W., and Smith, M.E. (1986). Predictors of food preferences in adult humans. *Appetite* 7, 109-125.

Lutz, R.J. (1975). Changing brand attitudes through modification of cognitive structure. *Journal of Consumer Research* 1, 49-59.

Lynch, J.G. (1979). Why additive models fail as descriptors of choice behavior. *Journal of Experimental Social Psychology* 15, 397-417.

Manstead, A.S.R., Proffitt, C., and Smart, J.L. (1983). Predicting and understanding mothers' infant-feeding intentions and behavior: Testing the theory of reasoned action. *Journal of Personality and Social Psychology* 44(4), 657-671.

Mattes, R.D., and Mela, D.J. (1986). Relationships between and among selected measures of sweet-taste preference and dietary intake. *Chemical Senses* 11(4), 523-539.

McGee, D., Rhoads, G., Hankin, J., Yano, K., and Tillotson, J. (1982). Within-person variability of nutrient intake in a group of Hawaiian men of Japanese ancestry. *American Journal of Clinical Nutrition* 36, 657-663.

Meiselman, H.L. (1986). Measurement of food habits in taste and smell disorders. In *Clinical measurement of taste and smell*, pp. 229-248. H.L. Meiselman, R.S. Rivlin (eds). New York: MacMillan Publishing Co.

Michela, J.L., and Contento, I.R. (1984). Spontaneous classification of foods by elementary school-aged children. *Health Education Quarterly* 11(1), 57-76.

Michela, J.L., and Contento, I.R. (1986). Cognitive, motivational, social, and environmental influences on children's food choices. *Health Psychology* 5(3), 209-230.

Moxley, R.L., and Wimberly, R.C. (1982). Dimensions of nutrition knowledge among preadolescent girls. *Home Economics Research Journal* 11, 41-46.

Netland, P.A., and Brownstein, H. (1984). Acculturation and the diet of Asian-American elderly. *Journal of Nutrition of the Elderly* 3(3), 37-56.

Newman, J.M., and Ludman, E.K. (1984). Chinese elderly: Food habits and beliefs. *Journal of Nutrition of the Elderly* 4(2), 3-13.

Nickols, S.Y., and Fox, K.D. (1983). Buying time and saving time: Strategies for managing household production. *Journal of Consumer Research* 10, 197-208.

Nickols, S.Y., and Metzen, E.J. (1978). Housework time of husband and wife. *Home Economics Research Journal* 7, 85-97.

Nunnally, J.C. (1978). *Psychometric theory.* New York: McGraw-Hill.

Ohlson, M.A., and Harper, L.J. (1976). Longitudinal studies of food intake and weight of women from ages 18 to 56 years. *Journal of The American Dietetic Association* 69, 626-631.

Ortiz, B., MacDonald, M., Ackerman, N., and Goebel, K. (1981). The effect of homemakers' employment on meal preparation time, meals at home, and meals away from home. *Home Economics Research Journal* 9, 200-206.

Osgood, C.E., Suci, G.J., and Tannenbaum, P.J. (1957). *The measurement of meaning.* Urbana, IL: University of Illinois Press.

Pennington, J.A.T. (1981). Considerations for a new food guide. *Journal of Nutrition Education* 13, 53-55.

Peterkin, B.B., Kerr, R.L., and Hama, M.Y. (1982). Nutritional adequacy of diets of low-income households. *Journal of Nutrition Education* 14, 102-104.

Phillips, D.E., Bass, M.A., and Yetley, E. (1978). Use of food and nutrition knowledge by mothers of preschool children. *Journal of Nutrition Education* 10, 73-75.

Pliner, P. (1982). The effects of mere exposure on liking for edible substances. *Appetite* 3, 283-290.

Pliner, P. (1983). Family resemblance in food preferences. *Journal of Nutrition Education* 15, 137-140.

Pliner, P., and Pelchat, M.L. (1986). Similarities in food preferences between children and their siblings and parents. *Appetite* 7, 333-342.

Popkin, B.M., and Haines, P.S. (1981). Factors affecting food selection: The role of economics. *Journal of The American Dietetics Association* 79, 419-425.

Price, D.W. (1982). Political economics of U.S. food and nutrition policy: Discussion. *American Journal of Agricultural Economics* 64, 1028-1029.

Randall, E. (1982). Food preferences as a determinant of food behavior. In *Social and cultural perspectives in nutrition* by D. Sanjur, pp. 123-146. Englewood Cliffs, NJ: Prentice-Hall, Inc.

Randall, E., and Sanjur, D. (1981). Food preferences--their conceptualization and relationship to consumption. *Ecology of Food and Nutrition* 11, 151-161.

Rathje, W.L. (1984). The garbage decade. In *Household refuse analysis: Theory, method, and applications in social science*, pp. 9-29. W.L. Rathje, C.K. Ritenbaugh (eds). Beverly Hills, CA: Sage Publications.

Redman, B.J. (1980). The impact of women's time allocation on food expenditure for meals away from home and prepared foods. *American Journal of Agricultural Economics* 62, 234-237.

Reilly, M.D. (1982). Working wives and convenience consumption. *Journal of Consumer Research* 8, 407-418.

Rizek, R.L., and Peterkin, B.B. (1979). Food costs of U.S. households, Spring 1977. *Family Economic Review* Fall, pp. 14-19.

Rosenthal, R. (1978). Combining results of independent studies. *Psychological Bulletin* 85, 185-193.

Rosenthal, R. (1982). Valid interpretation of qualitative research results. In *New directions for methodology of social and behavioral science: Forms of validity in research*, pp. 59-75. D. Brinberg, L. Kidder (eds). San Francisco: Jossey-Bass.

Rozin, P., and Cines, B.M. (1982). Ethnic differences in coffee use and attitudes to coffee. *Ecology of Food and Nutrition* 12, 79-88.

Rozin, P., and Millman, L. (1987). Family environment, not heredity, accounts for family resemblances in food preferences and attitudes: A twin study. *Appetite* 8, 125-134.

Rozin, P., and Vollmecke, T.A. (1986). Food likes and dislikes. *Annual Review of Nutrition* 6, 433-456.

Ryan, M.J. (1982). Behavioral intention formation: The interdependency of attitudinal and social influence variables. *Journal of Consumer Research* 7, 263-278.

Sadalla, E., and Burroughs, J. (1983). Profiles in eating: Sexy vegetarians and other diet-based social stereotypes. *Psychology Today* 15(10), 51-57.

Salathe, L.E. (1979). *Household expenditure patterns in the United States.* Tech. Bull. 1603. Washington, D.C.: U.S. Department of Agriculture.

Salathe, L.E., Gallo, A.E., and Boehm, W.T. (1979). *The impact of race on consumer food purchases.* Rep. No. ESCS-68. Washington, D.C.: U.S. Department of Agriculture.

Schafer, R.B., Reger, R.A., Gillespie, A.H., and Roderuck, C.E. (1980). Diet quality of selected samples of women and socio-demographic and social-psychological correlates. *Home Economics Research Journal* 8, 190-199.

Schiffman, S.S., Reynolds, M.L., and Young, F.W. (1981). *Introduction to multidimensional scaling.* New York: Academic Press.

Schmidt, F.L. (1973). Implications of a measurement problem for expectancy theory research. *Organizational Behavior and Human Performance* 10, 213-251.

Schorr, B.C., Sanjur, D., and Erickson, E.C. (1972). Teen-age food habits. *Journal of The American Dietetic Association* 61, 415-420.

Schutz, H.G., Moore, S.M., and Rucker, M.H. (1977). Predicting food purchase and use by multivariate attitudinal analysis. *Food Technology* 29(3), 50-64.

Schutz, H.G., Rucker, M.H., and Russell, G.F. (1975). Food and food-use classification systems. *Food Technology* 29(3), 50-64.

Schwartz, N.E. (1975). Nutrition knowledge, attitudes, and practices of high school graduates. *Journal of The American Dietetic Association* 66, 28-31.

Seiler, J., and Fox, H.M. (1973). Adolescent pregnancy: Association of dietary and obstetric factors. *Home Economics Research Journal* 1, 188-194.

Shepherd, R. (1987). The effects of nutritional beliefs and values on food acceptance. In *Food acceptance and nutrition*, pp. 387-402. J. Solms, D.A. Booth, R.M. Pangborn, O. Raunhardt (eds). San Diego, CA: Academic Press.

Shepard, R., and Stockley, L. (1987). Nutrition knowledge, attitudes, and fat consumption. *Journal of The American Dietetic Association* 87, 615-619.

Sims, L.S. (1978). Dietary status of lactating women. 2. Relation of nutritional knowledge and attitudes to nutrient intake. *Journal of The American Dietetic Association* 73, 147-154.

Sims, L.S. (1981). Toward an understanding of attitude measurement assessment in nutrition research. *Journal of The American Dietetic Association* 78, 460-466.

Skinner, J.D., Ezell, J.M., Salvetti, N.N., and Penfield, M.P. (1985). Relationship between mothers' employment and nutritional quality of adolescents' diets. *Home Economics Research Journal* 13, 18-25.

Smallwood, D., and Blaylock, J. (1981). *Impact of household size and income on food spending patterns*. Tech. Bull. 1650. Washington, D.C.: U.S. Department of Agriculture.

Smith, E.E., and Medin, D.L. (1981). *Categories and concepts*. Cambridge, MA: Harvard University Press.

Sobal, J., and Cassidy, C.M. (1987). Dieting foods: Conceptualizations and explanations. *Ecology of Food and Nutrition* 20, 89-96.

Stafford, K. (1983). The effects of wife's employment time on her household work. *Home Economics Research Journal* 11, 257-266.

Steinkamp, R.C., Cohen, N.L., and Walsh, H.E. (1965). Resurvey of aging population--Fourteen-year follow-up. The San Mateo Nutrition Study. *Journal of The American Dietetic Association* 46, 103-110.

Stone, H., and Sidel, J.L. (1985). *Sensory evaluation practices.* Orlando, FL: Academic Press.

Swagler, R.M. (1975). *Caveat emptor! An introductory analysis of consumer problems.* Lexington, MA: Heath.

Tong, A. (1986). Food habits of Vietnamese immigrants. *Family Economics Review* 2, 28-30.

Triandis, H.C. (1977). *Interpersonal behavior.* Monterey, CA: Brooks-Cole.

Tuorila, H. (1987a). Hedonic responses and attitudes in the acceptance of sweetness, saltiness and fattiness of foods. In *Food acceptance and nutrition*, pp. 337-351. J. Solms, D.A. Booth, R.M. Pangborn, O. Raunhardt (eds). San Diego, CA: Academic Press.

Tuorila, H. (1987b). Selection of milks with varying fat contents and related overall liking, attitudes, norms, and intentions. *Appetite* 8, 1-14.

Tuorila-Ollikainen, H., Lahteenmaki, L., and Salovaara, H. (1986). Attitudes, norms, intentions and hedonic responses in the selection of low salt bread in a longitudinal choice experiment. *Appetite* 7, 127-139.

Tversky, A., and Kahneman, D. (1974). Judgments under uncertainty: Heuristics and biases. *Science* 185, 1124-1131.

U.S. Department of Agriculture. Agriculture Research Service. (1957). *Essentials of an adequate diet--Facts for nutrition programs*, Homes Economics Research Report No. 3. Washington, D.C.: U.S. Department of Agriculture.

Waite, L.J. (1981). U.S. women at work. *Population Bulletin* 36(2), 1-43.

Wallendorf, M., and Reilly, M.D. (1983). Ethnic migration, assimilation, and consumption. *Journal of Consumer Research* 10, 292-302.

Webb, E.J., Campbell, D.T., Schwartz, R.D., Sechrest, L., and Grove, J.B. (1981). *Nonreactive measures in the social sciences.* Boston: Houghton-Mifflin.

Webster's New Collegiate Dictionary. (1979). Springfield, MA: G.&C. Merriam Co.

Wiggins, J.S. (1973). *Personality and prediction: Principles of personality assessment.* Reading, MA: Addison-Wesley.

Windham, C.T., Wyse, B.W., Hansen, R.G., and Hurst, R.L. (1983). Nutrient density of diets in the USDA Nationwide Food Consumption Survey, 1977-1978: I. Impact of socioeconomic status on dietary density. *Journal of The American Dietetic Association* 82, 28-34.

Windham, C.T., Wyse, B.W., Hurst, R.L., and Hansen, R.G. (1981). Consistency of nutrient consumption patterns in the United States. *Journal of The American Dietetic Association* 78, 587-595.

Woolcott, D.M., Kawash, G.F., and Sabry, J.H. (1981). Correlates of nutrition knowledge in Canadian businessmen. *Journal of Nutrition Education* 13, 153-156.

Wyant, K.W., and Meiselman, H.L. (1984). Sex and race differences in food preferences of military personnel. *Journal of The American Dietetic Association* 84, 169-175.

Yang, G.I., and Fox, H.M. (1979). Food habit changes of Chinese persons living in Lincoln, Nebraska. *Journal of The American Dietetic Association* 75, 420-424.

Yetley, E.A., and Roderuck, C. (1980). Nutritional knowledge and health goals of young spouses. *Journal of The American Dietetic Association* 77, 31-41.

Yperman, A.M., and Vermeersch, J.A. (1979). Factors associated with children's food habits. *Journal of Nutrition Education* 11, 72-76.

Zajonc, R.B. (1968). Attitudinal effects on mere exposure. *Journal of Personality and Social Psychology* 9(2, P.2), 1-27.

Zajonc, R.B., and Markus, H. (1982). Affective and cognitive factors in preferences. *Journal of Consumer Research* 9, 123-131.

Zimbardo, P.G., Ebbesen, E.B., and Maslach, C. (1977). *Influencing attitudes and changing behavior*. Reading, MA: Addison-Wesley Publishing Co.